Ethnography at Work

Ethnography at Work

Brian Moeran

Oxford • New York

First published in 2006 by
Berg
Editorial offices:
1st Floor, Angel Court, 81 St Clements Street, Oxford, OX4 1AW, UK
175 Fifth Avenue, New York, NY 10010, USA

Berg is the imprint of Oxford International Publishers Ltd.

Library of Congress Cataloging-in-Publication Data
Moeran, Brian, 1944-
   Ethnography at work / Brian Moeran.
      p. cm.
   Includes bibliographical references and index.
   ISBN-13: 978-1-84520-497-6 (cloth)
   ISBN-10: 1-84520-497-2 (cloth)
   1. Advertising agencies—Japan. 2. Advertising—Japan. 3.
Business anthropology—Japan. 4. Ethnology—Japan—Field
work. I. Title.

   HF6182.J3M636 2006
   659.1'11—dc22   2006017171

British Library Cataloguing-in-Publication Data
A catalogue record for this book is available from the British Library.

ISBN-13 978 184520 497 6 (Cloth)
ISBN-10 1 84520 497 2 (Cloth)

Typeset by Avocet Typeset, Chilton, Aylesbury, Bucks
Printed in the United Kingdom by Biddles Ltd, King's Lynn

www.bergpublishers.com

Contents

Acknowledgements

This book would never have been finished if I had not had the good fortune to be invited to spend a year as a visiting scholar at the National Museum of Ethnology, in Osaka, Japan. I am particularly indebted to its Director-General, Professor Makio Matsuzono, for issuing the formal invitation, and to Professor Hirochika Nakamaki who acted as my mentor-cum-minder during my stay and showered me with goodwill, good advice, good introductions and good conversation during the year.

I am also very grateful to many other members of the staff of the Museum – both academic and administrative – for their varied forms of assistance and support: Hirose Kōjirō, Kondō Tomoko, Peter Matthews, Morikage Tomomi, Okajima Reiko, Yamamoto Sayoko and Yoneyama Yukako.

Last, but not least, of course, I owe an immense debt of gratitude to all those working in Asahi Tsūshinsha, as the advertising agency was then called, for the goodwill, patience and care with which they helped me during my fieldwork there.

Preface

Two separate events encouraged me to write this book.

The first occurred when I was a visiting professor at the Copenhagen Business School. Soon after I arrived, I was asked by a colleague to give a two-hour lecture on advertising in Japan in a general course on management that she was co-ordinating for final-year undergraduate students. I asked what exactly she wished me to talk about, and was advised in rather vague terms to tell them about my experiences as an ethnographer in a Japanese advertising agency.

This I duly did. As part of my explanation of how people in the advertising agency interact both among themselves and with the client (or advertiser) and other players in the industry, I told the two dozen students present about an account team's preparations for a competitive presentation for a client. Before I was halfway through my story, one student interrupted and said dismissively, 'This is just a case study, isn't it?'

That certainly brought my middle-aged loquaciousness to a jarring halt (no bad thing in itself!). Having paused for thought, I tried to explain the general significance to be drawn from the particulars described, but my interlocutor was unimpressed. A case was just a case: a practical example that was no more than a practical example, to be discussed, analysed and cast aside for the next case. It had no general significance. I disagreed, but was not well enough prepared to argue my case coherently and persuasively there and then (I came back to it later on in the class). Unimpressed, my interlocutor and his fellow students then asked me to talk about something else more immediately pertinent to their interest in Japanese management. (We were in Denmark where an egalitarian ethos demands that there be no status differences between people, even though there may be clear signs thereof.)

The second 'event' has been repeated several times since I started writing about the Japanese advertising world more than a decade ago now. From time to time, I have written a paper and submitted it to a non-anthropological journal for consideration for publication. As is customary with academic submissions of this nature, each paper has been sent out to anonymous reviewers whose comments on its contents have then been relayed to me. On each occasion, my reviewers have tended to adopt very different standpoints regarding the strengths, weaknesses and potential directions I might take in the rewriting of the paper for eventual publication in the journal concerned.

What gradually became clear from these experiences is that, because I am an anthropologist who likes to include a case study based on fieldwork in his writings, the sheer richness of the material leads to a plurality of opinions about what theories would best suit how such material should be interpreted. This has, however, led to authorial confusion. Should I follow Reviewer A, who thinks that I need to locate the paper within specific readings in economic sociology, for example? Or Reviewer B, who is adamant that Japanese culture presents a 'special case' of which I have failed to take account? Or Reviewer C, who wonders whether the paper, because it deals with advertising, should not tackle the literature on creative clusters?

Not surprisingly, perhaps, the divergence of scholarly opinion has also led to editorial confusion. My submissions have clearly not fitted into editors' standardized expectations of what is and is not publishable in the reputable scholarly journals for which they are responsible. One poor soul was still unable to make up her mind about whether to publish one of my papers after she had commissioned six different reviewers to read it! Another was brave enough to publish my rewritten submission that ignored all three theoretical tangents suggested by reviewers of the initial manuscript and went off on a (quite novel) fourth tack. For all the attention that is now paid by our administrative masters to citation indices and journal ratings, I have found publishing in academic journals to be very much a hit-and-miss, luck-of-the-draw affair. Fortunately, I am old and senior enough these days not to need to worry myself too much over the outcome of my submissions. But my heartfelt sympathies go to my younger colleagues who are not so fortunate.

So, what is 'just a case study' for some people clearly poses considerable theoretical problems for others. Indeed, one of the advantages I have gained from these review processes has been an insight into new ways that I might develop the same ethnographic material. It is this insight that has prompted the writing of this book.

What I have done here is simple. After briefly outlining a few of the issues that interest me with regard to casework and ethnographic research, I present a detailed account of my participation in a Japanese advertising agency's preparations for a competitive presentation to be made to a global Japanese corporate client. Having laid out the detail, I then proceed to ask six different sets of theoretical questions of the material.

- What *is* an account and how does the way in which money is distributed within the advertising industry affect the organization of its main players – advertisers, media and agencies?
- Why are advertiser accounts surrounded by stories and what do these and other stories tell us about the structure and organization of an advertising agency and the field of advertising in which it operates?
- How do advertising agencies – and, by corollary, other corporations – convince

potential partners of their professionalism through what Erving Goffman has called 'impression management'?

- What is the nature of 'creativity' in an advertising agency? How are creative ideas arrived at in advertising campaigns and what kinds of conditions constrain copywriters and art designers in their work? How do the practices of creativity affect agency organization and why?

- Is it targeted consumers who are the focus of an account team's attention, or is it client personnel who form the 'other' in the world of advertising? What happens when consumers are foreign? How are they 'imagined' and why?

- How did I get involved in the competitive presentation in the first place, and what does ethnography as a methodology tell us that other methodologies can't tell us about business organization in general? Is there ultimately any difference between anthropologists and corporate managers when it comes to doing ethnography?

These six different, though interlocking, strands of theoretical inquiry all stem from the single case study presented. It is only by radically contextualizing theoretical issues in fieldwork material that we can begin to make sense of a business field. And what I try to show is that there is no single 'sense', but numerous different 'senses' that result. If nothing else, *Ethnography At Work* advertises the fact that ethnography – that is, a detailed ethnography of work – really works.

Brian Moeran
National Museum of Ethnology, Osaka

Part I
The Case

–1–

It's in the Name

The case study presented here comes from the world of Japanese advertising and details preparations by a large advertising agency for a presentation in which it had been invited to compete, along with one other agency, by a major Japanese electronics multinational. The name of the agency was Asahi Tsūshinsha, or Asatsu, at the time ranked as the sixth largest agency in Japan. Now, thanks to further growth and a strategic merger with another large agency, it is called ADK and is the third in the rankings – after Dentsu, the world's largest single agency, and Hakuhodo.

Some years ago, I was given permission to carry out an ethnographic study of Asatsu. The simple question underlying my research was as follows. Scholars in the fields of cultural studies, sociology and anthropology had spent – and still spend – a lot of time using semiotic, feminist and other forms of analysis to critically dissect finished advertisements.[1] But nobody seemed to consider how advertisements came to be made in the first place. By shifting scholarly emphasis from the reception of advertisements as *products* to the social *processes* involved in the production of advertising, I hoped to be able to answer the question of how and why advertisements are as they are. Why are particular images selected over others? What are the alternatives that are discarded, and why? What are the marketing aims behind an advertising campaign and how are these reflected in the final product? What are the processes of negotiation that take place among those involved in the creation of newspaper and magazine print advertisements, radio and television commercials, billboard hoardings, retail outlet posters, transport ads, and so on?

I was extremely lucky in my choice of agency (more of the hows and whys of this later on in the book). Those concerned gave me virtually free rein during my year's stay in Asatsu, although formally I was allocated to a different division during each month of my research – starting with the President's Office, and then moving through Media Buying, Marketing, Account Services, Creative, Promotions, International, Personnel and other divisions. In this way, I was able to get an all-round view of the agency's varied activities, from strategic market development to the production of animated cartoons, by way of personnel training, location shoots, and the production of one ad campaign that I followed through from start to finish.[2]

As a researcher, of course, I faced difficulties from time to time, but those around me usually did their very best to accommodate my requests and answer my sometimes wayward questions. One difficulty that became particularly problematic after two or three months of fieldwork concerned agency-client relationships. Given the confidential nature of clients' marketing and advertising strategies, how was I ever going to be able to witness the dozens and dozens of meetings and negotiations that took place daily between Asatsu staff and employees of the companies which had retained the agency to carry out their advertising needs? Moreover, how could I possibly manage to be present at one of those secretive occasions when Asatsu made what is called a 'presentation' to a client or would-be client?

In the advertising industry, a presentation is a performance put on by an agency to demonstrate its unique skills in marketing analysis and creative ideas and so to persuade an advertiser to contract the agency to carry out its advertising over a period of time. In a way, preparing for a presentation is a kind of foreplay preceding a more serious relationship between agency and client. This much I now know. But three months into my research, which was when events in this chapter occurred, things were much less clear.

Because I was at the time assigned to the Account Services Division, and because a senior manager, whom I shall call Yano, had taken me under his wing during my stay there, I decided to broach the issue with Yano. He heard me out and agreed that my participation in one of Asatsu's presentations might indeed be difficult. 'Still, leave it with me, *sensei*,' he said reassuringly, using the polite term of 'teacher' by which he always called me to show his respect for someone who at the time occupied a chair professorship at the University of London. 'I'll see what can be done.'[3]

The story that follows came about because Yano was not only true to his word, but actually arranged for me to be present at a presentation when Asatsu competed with an incumbent agency for the account of a large Japanese multinational, which I shall here call by the pseudonym of Frontier. It was the fact that, by good luck and a little engineering on Yano's part, I was able not only to observe, but also to participate actively in, preparations leading up to a presentation that provided me with the bases for the theoretical insights that I intend to develop in the following chapters.

Orientation

One April, at the start of a new corporate year,[4] the International Division of Frontier's headquarters in Tokyo asked its contracted agency, J&M, to prepare an advertising campaign that would elevate its brand image in both the United States and Germany. At the same time, because Asatsu was already successfully handling one of Frontier's domestic accounts, and because certain people in the client company were not entirely satisfied with the work currently being done by J&M, Frontier's International Division invited Asatsu to participate in what thus became a competitive presentation.

In its orientation to Asatsu, Frontier explained that it had decided to manage its overall marketing strategy by three broad geographical areas: America, Europe and Asia. Its sales covered a broad range of products: laser disc software, computer CD-ROMs, CD players, multi-cassette players, projection TV sets, car navigation systems and so on. Some of these (e.g. laser disc players) were better established in the United States than they were in Europe.

Three problems had to be dealt with by the two agencies participating in the presentation. First of all, many consumers saw no fundamental differences in the qualities of the *products* put out by Frontier and its competitors. Secondly, there was a challenge to the company's *brand image* in the sense that, even though it was the originator of laser technology, Frontier was not perceived by consumers to be as technologically advanced as Sony and was as a result in danger of being dismissed as a 'mini Sony'. Thirdly, *the market* suggested that Frontier's targeted consumers were older and fewer in number than Sony's customers, although it was hoped that the reunification of Germany and the unification of Europe (EU) would help the company rejuvenate its overall brand image in Europe, if not the US. Frontier's own marketing research suggested that there was considerable potential for growth in the expanding rental markets, accompanied by a corresponding expansion in the distribution of software, in both the US and Germany.

Following this orientation, Asatsu set up an account team or group headed by an account manager, Ueda, whose job it was to liaise closely with the client company's personnel and to co-ordinate marketing, creative and media-buying activities within Asatsu during the period leading up to the presentation. He was joined by a couple of other account executives, one of whom had previously worked on another Frontier account handled by the agency and who could thus provide valuable input regarding the client's overall marketing and sales strategies, as well as what was known about Frontier's back-stage power relations. The account group also consisted of a marketing team of three people who were expected to analyse all the data provided by the client, carry out surveys of their own as necessary, and come up with a marketing strategy that fitted the brief provided by Frontier. Then there was a media buyer or planner who worked out which newspapers, what kind of magazines, and what sort of programmes aired by television and radio stations would be most suited to Frontier's proposed ad campaign and target audience in terms of all sorts of criteria ranging from demographics and psychographics, on the one hand, to reach, CPM (cost per mille, i.e. cost of advertising per thousand viewers), and so on, on the other. Finally, but by no means least of all, there was a creative team composed of creative director, copywriters and art directors whose job was to transform market analysis into visual images and language.

This was a comparatively large account team. Normally, domestic accounts were handled by one or two account executives, a two-man marketing team overseen by a manager, and a creative team of copywriter and art director overseen by a creative director. In this case, however, Asatsu felt that it was worth investing more manpower in preparations for the competitive presentation. After all, Frontier was a big-name Japanese multinational. Winning one of its prestigious, or 'blue chip', accounts would confer considerable status on Asatsu itself, and that was very important for an agency intent on moving up the rankings from sixth to third largest advertising agency in Japan.

When the account team as a whole first met, it was generally agreed that they had to take account of, and somehow get across to consumers, a number of related points to meet the challenges outlined by Frontier in its orientation. These included the reliability and high quality of Frontier's products, its strength and innovation in audio-visual and laser technology, and the idea of entertainment as a means towards enriching consumers' lives. Ideally this 'aspirational value' would be reinforced by a unified campaign that emphasized *one brand, one voice* in its creative ideas.

To achieve all these aims, the account team recognized that Frontier had to address two main target audiences. One was an *outer audience group*, consisting of 20- and 30-year-old men and women in Germany and the US, who were in an upper-middle socio-economic bracket. It also included those who already owned entertainment-oriented VTR players, and were influential in the development of information technology, as well as steady, rather than just trend-conscious, consumers. The other was an *inner audience group*, employed in Frontier itself, at its headquarters in Tokyo, as well as at sales outlets and in branch offices abroad in Germany and the US. It also included those working on Frontier accounts in American and German advertising agencies.[5]

Under the leadership of the account manager, Ueda, the account team arrived at an overall campaign strategy that combined a number of different elements. The campaign's immediate external purpose was to improve Frontier's corporate image, brand prestige and aspirational value. Its mid- to long-term aim was to create a unified global umbrella brand image (*one brand, one voice*) that would cover particular product advertising campaigns in individual countries around the world. Its internal purpose was to boost morale within the client company and ensure that employees appreciated the initiative being taken by headquarters management in creating Frontier's new image strategy.

Brand Concept and Pre-presentation

Having arrived at this analysis of the market and Frontier's position therein, the account team needed to come up with a basic brand concept, corporate slogan and communication strategy that included one or more sets of print advertisements illustrating the approach it was proposing that Frontier adopt. The problem here – as in all advertising campaigns – was how to transform market analysis into creative ideas. It was here that as an anthropologist I was brought into the game.

As part of my fieldwork in Asatsu, as I mentioned at the beginning of the chapter, I was placed in different divisions dealing with different spheres of the agency's activities – print media buying, television advertising, marketing, merchandising, and so on – for a month at a time in order to learn how employees went about their jobs. In due course, I found myself in the Accounts Services Division, a particularly opaque part of the agency because of the extremely intimate relations developed by account executives[6] with their opposite numbers (product managers, advertising managers, directors, and so on) in client companies. I had heard about the existence of presentations, but had little idea of when or where or how often they took place; of who attended them, or of what they consisted of in substance.

A couple of weeks after I had mentioned this difficulty to Yano, the Head of the Account Services Division, and we had agreed that this part of the agency's business might be difficult to observe because of the recurrent problem of 'client confidentiality', I received a phone call from Yano at home late one evening.

'*Sensei*,' he began apologetically, in his customarily unctuous voice. 'I *do* hope I didn't get you out of bed. No? Oh, that's a relief. You see, I'm phoning to ask for your help.'

Me? Help? Doing my best to hold down my excitement, I reassured him that I was still very much awake and asked what I could do to help. Yano briefly outlined the situation: Asatsu had been asked to make a presentation in English to a Japanese client for both its German and American markets. Could I, as a native English speaker, a European, and someone with experience of the United States, possibly be kind enough to help out by checking the English and giving my opinion of the ads that had been prepared by the creative team?

Was this the opportunity I had been looking for? I quickly acceded to Yano's request and at half past eight the following morning, a Friday, found myself being taken to one of the agency's small, windowless meeting rooms. There I was introduced briefly to half a dozen men – all smoking and gazing at several large placards on the tables in front of them. Boards with ads by rival companies were placed on a thin shelf along one wall of the room in front of me. The account manager, Ueda, proceeded to give me a brief orientation (as described in greater detail above) and then asked me to give my opinion of six series of ads prepared by the creative team for a 'pre-presentation' to one of the Frontier managers that same afternoon. The real pitch was to take place the following Tuesday.

After I had asked a few questions for clarification, Ueda's colleagues from the creative team showed me several series of mock-ups, all with headlines, dummy copy,[7] the client's name and slogan. I soon gathered that each series – each consisting of three ads – was named, to enable recognition during the course of the account team's discussions. The series were:

1. Perspiration – consisting of stark black and white photographs of perspiring musicians (a flamenco dancer, jazz drummer and classical violinist).
2. Nature – using slightly greenish-grey tinted photographs of what was almost certainly an American desert.
3. Home Entertainment – depicting various combinations of laser and compact disc outlines with photographs of different entertainers performing.
4. Musicians – focusing on close-up photos of three men with musical instruments.
5. Young Women – featuring attractive young models asking which company made the first laser disc player and other Frontier products.
6. Creativity Quotient – taking its title from one of the series' headlines.

I did my best to comment on each. The Perspiration series might do better in Germany than in the US since it seemed to be aimed more at 'intellectual' than ordinary music lovers. Also, *Performance* (or *dance*) *is my soul's voice* might be a better headline than *Music is my soul's voice* for the flamenco dancer, if only to avoid repetition of the word 'music' that was being used for the picture of the classical musician. The Young Women ads seemed fairly sexist (one model was standing by a doorway with a come-on look that reminded me of London prostitutes back in the 1960s) and might therefore cause offence. Both the Nature and Musicians series had some 'Orientalist' headlines that were styled as if they were *haiku* poems (*Nature speaks / loudest / when silent* and *A month of filming / five minutes / on the screen*). These would probably appeal to Japanese – in particular, the Nature ads – but I was not convinced that they would persuade the targeted American and German consumers of Frontier's merits. The Creativity Quotient series I found hard to grasp. Ad mock-ups showed Jimi Hendrix with his guitar; Walt Disney with a drawing of Mickey Mouse; and Orson Welles gazing down at Citizen Kane on stage (described in the body copy as the 'Kane Mutiny'!). What was the connection? Each picture, one of the creative team replied, showed Frontier's pioneering spirit. Was it a spirit, then, that existed only in the past?

The Frontier tag line, too, caught my attention: *The Pulse of Entertainment*. I asked how and why this phrase was being used, but was told that it had been provided by Frontier itself at its orientation two weeks previously. A second choice was *The Art of Entertainment*. A third alternative, much liked by a senior Frontier director, was *The Light of Joy and Creativity*. None of these taglines seemed entirely right for the client's needs and aims.

By this time it was nearing midday, and Ueda and his colleagues pressed me to say which series I liked best. I went for the Perspiration series, mainly because of the immediate effect of the stark, black-and-white visuals of the flamenco dancers, jazz drummer and classical violinist, but I knew that this was a choice based on a combination of personal cosmopolitan eclecticism and white, (upper?) middle-class taste. The Home Entertainment series seemed to be direct and to the point – something that both Americans and Germans might appreciate.[8] The Creativity Quotient series was interesting, but not immediately understandable in the context of Frontier's *future*-oriented marketing strategy.

At this point, Yano came back into the room to see how things were getting on. The copywriter went off to order lunch, while the art director was busy amending the English mistakes that I had noted and doing an efficient cut-and-paste job to the mock-ups' headlines. Yano and Ueda conferred quietly in a corner, before the former turned to me and said, *'Sensei*, I have been talking with Ueda here and he has agreed to let you sit in on this afternoon's pre-presentation as part of your research.' He then left with a smile, as I mumbled my effusive thanks.

The pre-presentation took place at two o'clock in a room that was soon pretty cramped, but which at least had a window in it. All sorts of people – some of them unexpected – turned up for the occasion including: three members of Frontier's International Division, and, from Asatsu, its account team; a creative team from its international subsidiary (including an American copywriter, who had worked on one or two – but not all – of the series); the head of the Account Services Division handling the Frontier domestic account (Yano); the head of the International Division (which, if Asatsu won the presentation, would handle the new foreign account); the agency's executive director and vice-president; and myself. During the best part of the following two hours, Ueda, the marketing team director and creative director explained Asatsu's overall marketing and communications strategies that it intended to propose to its client. There were some sharp questions from Tanaka, the chief Frontier executive present, who asked Ueda to explain, for example, why it was using red rather than standard blue for his company's logo; and why it had not made use of the *Light of Joy and Creativity* tagline, even though it had been emphasized by the managing director of Frontier at the agency's orientation three weeks previously. He asked more detailed questions about Asatsu's media plan and budgeting, before wondering how the six series of ads presented were to be taken. Was the agency going to recommend a particular approach? Or was it going to leave Frontier to fumble around on its own (in Tanaka's opinion a fatal strategy)?

Ueda was clearly at a loss. Hesitating a few long seconds, he finally suggested that Asatsu would recommend the Perspiration series – followed by the Creativity Quotient series with Jimi Hendrix and his guitar. Tanaka did not seem that impressed. Wouldn't the Home Entertainment series benefit sales, and the Nature ads help Frontier's corporate image? Perhaps Asatsu should check consumer reactions to these series by Tuesday? Moreover the agency had made no attempt to distinguish between American and German cultural differences. This was a problem for Frontier's head office, which needed back-up reasoning to persuade its staff that whatever choices it made were right.

Post-Mortem and Strategy

It was late afternoon when Tanaka and his colleagues took their leave. Once they had been seen off at the elevators, everyone reassembled in the same room for a post-mortem. This kind of meeting, as I was to learn later, was almost always held after visits from clients to Asatsu and was, in a way, a performance about the earlier performance of the pre-presentation. It was extremely important because, firstly, all those present could give their own personal interpretations and assessments of what had gone on in the meeting with the client. Secondly, they could then form a strategy for further action. And, thirdly, the meeting gave them the opportunity to discuss and analyse the organizational structure of their client's company.[9] These three activities together contributed towards Asatsu's ultimate ability to demonstrate to a potential client that it was a credible and professional organization which could be entrusted with servicing an advertiser's needs.

In this particular meeting, the head of the International Division started the discussion, since – if the presentation were successful – the account would be handled by his division. Picking up on something Tanaka had hinted at, he said that the presentation itself had been too fragmented and that one speaker was needed, not three. There was general agreement on this, and he proceeded to designate the account team leader, Ueda, as Asatsu's single presenter to ensure continuity and coherence in the presentation argument (*one brand, one voice!*).

Yano then stepped in as head of the division handling one of Frontier's domestic accounts and commented that the competing agency, J&M, would almost certainly take along at least one foreigner to its presentation. In his opinion, Asatsu had to do the same, if it was to seem credibly international. Several people nodded their heads in agreement. But, Yano continued, the American copywriter had to be in Chicago the following Tuesday on another job, so he was wondering whether it might be appropriate to invite me to act as Asatsu's foreign 'spokesman' at the presentation. Again, people nodded their heads. I was thus formally appointed as a subsidiary member of the account team. Yano had found an opportunity to meet with my request and my participant-observation was now legitimated as part of Asatsu's preparations for the big event the following Tuesday.

The next question concerned the client's organization. Who was the account team's target man in Frontier? Yano needed to know who was going to have the greatest say in whether Asatsu was, or was not, chosen to represent Frontier in

Germany and the United States. Ueda quickly mentioned the name of Frontier's managing director, Oba, adding that it was he who was keen on the idea of 'light' as an overall concept. Yano then said that he would use his networks to try to find a way to talk informally to Oba and make him better predisposed to select Asatsu to handle the Frontier account.[10]

The head of the International Division took over once more. The pre-presentation had made it clear that Asatsu must decide which ads Oba was likely to approve or disapprove of and to make its selection accordingly. As presenter, Ueda, too, had to know in his own mind why Asatsu was not adopting Oba's tag line, *The Light of Joy and Creativity*.

There followed a long, practical discussion about each of the series presented. Some of this concerned copyright and permissions, but most focused on the six advertising campaign series the creative team had prepared. Of these, the Nature series aroused most controversy. Many of those Japanese present liked it, but the two foreigners (the American copywriter and myself) in the room expressed their reservations: primarily because it mimicked what seemed to them to be a pseudo-*haiku* poetic style. Headlines may have followed a tripartite structure, but they made no use of the kind of allusion and suggestiveness traditionally adhered to by Japanese *haiku* poets. The Musicians series was put aside, as was the Young Women series to which Tanaka had reacted rather like myself since he had been overheard muttering 'prostitution' to one of his colleagues. This left us with the Creativity Quotient and Home Entertainment series. The latter seemed more promising, given Tanaka's parting words and its obvious product sales advantage. Could its design be altered somehow to fit in with the Perspiration series and so enable Asatsu to propose 'Phase 1' and 'Phase 2' stages in its presentation the following Tuesday? With a bit of playing around (first, by peeling off some letters down one side of one series), design-wise they were made to resemble each other. But Ueda expressed some unease about the idea of phases, even though it was clearly important for Frontier. He would need to provide a rationale for them – starting with a broad theme, perhaps, before narrowing down to particulars – in order to justify why Asatsu had selected these two particular series of ads.

At this point, the account executive in charge of Frontier's domestic account, already handled by Asatsu, was called to the phone. Someone somewhere in the agency had already been in touch with Tanaka who had been more than pleased with the Perspiration and Nature series. Still, J&M were due to make their pre-presentation the following Monday, so maybe a final decision should be postponed until we heard what had gone on there.[11]

In the meantime, action needed to be taken on the tag lines. *The Pulse of Entertainment* should be checked in the US by the American copywriter once he got there. He should also try to get Americans' feedback on *The Light of Joy and Creativity*, since this was so close to Oba's heart. Maybe he should include tag lines used by competitors – like Sony's *The One and Only* – when gauging American reactions. My job was to get resident foreigners' opinions of all the tag lines, as well as an overall ranking of each of the series, including comments on visuals, headlines, body copy (where used), design and total impact. Did the separate elements in each of the series interconnect? Did people actually shift from visual to headline to body copy to tag line? If so, why? And what did they think of Frontier as a result? Meanwhile, half a dozen forty-year-old American men with artificial suntans waiting outside in the corridor to audition for a television commercial were brought in and asked for their – as it turned out inconclusive – opinions of the ads propped up against the walls of our meeting room.

Post-rationalization and Creative Justification

That evening I talked about the tag lines with a group of friends. Not one of them liked *The Pulse of Entertainment*. One – in a passable imitation of Laurence Olivier as Henry V at Agincourt – suggested *To the Frontiers*. Another – who worked in the fashion industry – said that the trouble with Frontier was that it was too frightened of being forthright. 'Like its name says,' she said, 'it should be a cutting-edge company.' This helped me latch onto the tag lines *Like the Name Says* and *It's (all) in the Name*. While I sipped my beer, I also scrawled down another phrase that leapt to mind: *Entertaining Ideas for the Future*.

Advertising often advances by means of *post*-rationalization. If I was going to persuade Ueda that my ideas were of any use, I needed to justify them. So I found myself later that night trying to explain *It's (All) in the Name* to myself in terms of certain principles in structural linguistics that I had read many years previously. The marketing of products and the meanings they took on, I reasoned, seemed no different in principle from the Swiss linguist Ferdinand de Saussure's discussion of how 'the value of any given word is determined by what other words there are in that particular area of the vocabulary.'[12] Thus every product (Walkman or Discman, video or tape recorder, laser or compact disc) took on meaning in association with those other products with which it was marketed. Moreover, there was a parallel between products and their manufacturers, on the one hand, and syntagmatic and associative relations in language, on the other.[13] Products might be made by the same or different manufacturers, in series that were related to one another diachronically (different versions of a VTR player put out over time by Frontier) or synchronically across space (simultaneously competing VTR players manufactured by Frontier, on the one hand, and by Sony, Hitachi, National, GE, Phillips and so on, on the other). Together, like components of a language, they formed a system.

In this way, I convinced myself that I had my post-rationalized theory for my ideas. The following morning I called Ueda up and explained how Frontier needed to set itself apart from its competitors by ensuring that its tag line did not have any associations with those of rival companies. *The Art of Entertainment* ran into trouble with Aiwa's *The Art of Aiwa*, while any allusion to the 'future' would run foul of JVC's *Founders of the Future*, and a focus on technology would clash with Sanyo's *The New Wave in Japanese Technology*. By focussing on 'entertainment', I reasoned, Frontier would merely be falling in line with a set of associations (art, technology, future) that did not really differentiate one company from another, in the way that Sony had been able to do with its *The One and Only*. Frontier needed to be incomparable. It had to adopt a tag line that was distinctive and timeless, not subject to fashion. By going for something like *It's (All) in the Name*, *The Name Says it (All)* or *Like the Name Says*, Frontier would be able to re-enforce its image and turn back on itself in a never-ending cycle. Frontier produced cutting edge products at the 'frontier' – a descriptive noun that was also the company's name, and so on ad infinitum. In short, *Frontier = Frontier*.

Ueda listened politely, but did not sound particularly enthusiastic. I had the distinct impression that he had a sound grasp of both the theory and practice of structural linguistics and had already done this kind of reasoning for himself. Nevertheless, he asked me to write everything down for a Monday morning meeting. In the meantime, I tried to get friends' reactions to the ad series dreamed up by the creative team, and added my own tag line for comment among the others given to Asatsu by Frontier. Although there was no clear-cut favourite so far as the series were concerned (the Perspiration and Creativity Quotient ads were generally preferred to the Nature and Home Entertainment series), a resounding majority of the two dozen or so people I asked picked out *Like the Name Says* and/or *It's in the Name* as their preferred tag line (provided I drop the *all*).

On Monday morning I presented my findings to Ueda who was by then preoccupied with other urgent matters. The creative people had been working through the weekend day and night, trying to get everything right. The media planner had been faxing back and forth between Tokyo and Asatsu offices in Los Angeles and Frankfurt, getting the necessary information on costs, reach, frequency, gross impression and the other imponderables of audience reception. These would enable Ueda to answer difficult questions about the campaign budget at the presentation the following afternoon. All I could do, it seemed, was point out one or two spelling mistakes and misprints, so I went off and did other things about the agency. Maybe I had been a bit over-optimistic about my own potential usefulness as both foreigner and academic in the preparations for the Frontier campaign.

Presentation

Or had I? The next afternoon we took a train down to Frontier's headquarters in Meguro, loaded with slide and overhead projectors, a couple of dozen bound copies of the presentation proposal, ad story boards, and so on. The client had assigned a room on the top floor of its office normally used only by the company's Board of Directors, with an anteroom for the performers to prepare in and retire to. Asatsu fielded ten people all told (three of them senior executive directors who had not been involved in preparations for the presentation), while Frontier brought in almost two dozen – ranging from senior executives to middle- and low-ranking managers. We sat along one side of a long oval table, they along the other and at the end of the boardroom. Proceedings began with the usual greetings on each side, and the reason for our being there together was made clear before Ueda was invited to give his 'pitch'.

He started off on points made in Frontier's orientation to Asatsu, moved to a market analysis and then embarked upon the agency's proposed communication strategy. Making use of slides, he outlined the 'inner' and 'outer' target audiences, the campaign aims and basic brand concept, *Towards New Frontiers in Entertainment*, before shifting to a discussion of the tag line. After outlining reasons for adopting *The Pulse of Entertainment*, he suddenly flashed on the screen as an alternative, *Entertaining Ideas for the Future*. My tag line, he said – without attributing authorship – had been very favourably received in the United States because it attracted one's attention,[14] gave off an impression of creativity, resonated well, was future oriented and suitable for entertainment-related products.

Ueda then introduced a new slide proposing a second series of tag lines – *Like the Name Says*, *The Name Says it All* and *It's in the Name* – under the umbrella concept of *Frontier = Frontier*. He proceeded to justify Asatsu's reasoning along precisely the Saussurean lines that I had used over the phone to him the previous Saturday morning.

The creative recommendations that followed were divided into 'depth' (*Frontier = Frontier*) and 'scope' (*Entertaining Ideas for the Future*) approaches (that were more or less the kind of 'phases' discussed at the post-mortem meeting). The Perspiration series was recommended for the depth approach (with *Performance is my Soul's Voice* as the headline for the visual of the flamenco dancer), and the Nature series as back-up. For its 'scope' approach, Asatsu recommended the Home Entertainment and Creativity Quotient series in that order. Noticing my surprise, the head of the International Division, who was sitting beside me, leant over and whispered in my ear in English, 'Very good ideas, *sensei*!'

But would they be good enough to persuade Frontier to choose Asatsu over its rival, J&M? We found out soon enough. Just after lunch the next day, Yano told me to go over to the International Division's building at three o'clock. Tanaka was due to come and inform us officially that Frontier had decided to award Asatsu its international account. I duly presented myself and joined the rest of the account team on the ninth floor. Tanaka arrived, accompanied by Ueda, the head of the International Division, and Yano, and was seated on one side of the long oval table that was usually reserved for presentations made by the agency on its home turf. We were lined up on the other side. Formal greetings were exchanged and Tanaka, in a far more relaxed mood than we had previously seen him, went straight to the point. Frontier had decided to ask Asatsu to act as the agency responsible for its German and North American advertising markets. After due noises of gratitude were expressed by managerial and account team staff, Tanaka continued by saying that those present at the two presentations the previous afternoon had been involved in lengthy discussions over the de/merits of each of the agencies' proposals. Two things had had to be decided: the brand concept and tag line, on the one hand; and the communication strategy and ad campaigns to be used, on the other.

While younger members of Frontier had been more inclined to support J&M's vision of *Power Technology*, older members had felt that Asatsu's Perspiration and Home Entertainment series were closer to Frontier's vision. However, all agreed that the agency had *potential* and it was this potential – exhibited in its ability to come up with new tag lines in particular – which decided Frontier to award Asatsu its account. The 'pitch', too, had been a contributing factor and Tanaka commented favourably on how Ueda had clearly given everything to the presentation – so much so that he had more or less collapsed upon finishing.

Tanaka then turned to the question of the tag line. Apparently everyone present had agreed that the tag line to go for was *It's in the Name*. This, they felt, expressed exactly what Frontier was all about. But those at the top – including Oba who was keen on his 'light' idea – had felt that it was perhaps a couple of decades ahead of its time and too close in concept to Sony's *The One and Only*. The last thing Frontier wanted was to be seen as a 'mini' Sony. So, reluctantly, they had decided to shelve *It's in the Name* for the time being. Instead, it was agreed that they should go for *The Art of Entertainment*, turn down all communication strategy ideas and ask Asatsu to come up with a new ad campaign.

Questions

What are we to make of this description of an ad agency's preparations for a campaign presentation to a potential client? Those of you interested in the everyday world of business relations will have noted, I suspect, several intriguing points in my writing of this case study. These will probably have made you pause to consider a number of different, interrelated questions that will be covered, and hopefully answered, in the remaining chapters of this book.

1. Up to the time of the presentation, Frontier was contracting at least two agencies to handle different parts of its advertising appropriation. Why does a corporation or client in Japan contract more than one advertising agency to handle its advertising and promotional strategies? Don't issues of client confidentiality

arise? What are the advantages and disadvantages of this method of distributing a company's advertising budget among different agencies? And how does it affect relations within an ad agency, as well as between agency and client? Are there broader economic, social and organizational ramifications within the industry as a whole?

2. The planning of Asatsu's presentation to Frontier involved an awful lot of meetings and discussions of one sort or another. What is the function of all the talk that goes on between account manager, account executives, marketing analysts, creative director, copywriters, art directors, media buyers and senior management (not to mention the foreign anthropologist)? What kind of talk takes place, between whom, when, where and why? How do the stories that emerge reflect the social organization of an advertising agency, agency-client relations and the advertising industry as a whole? Why and how are ad campaigns themselves transformed into stories about products?

3. Preparations for the presentation also revealed a set of clear, but to many people invisible, relations between particular individuals in the potential client corporation and the agency seeking to win its advertising account. How are these individual relations established, and for what purpose? How are they transformed into institutional relations? An advertising agency has to persuade a (would-be) client that it is best suited for the job in hand. What kind of communicative strategies do company personnel adopt in order to achieve this aim? How do they manage individual and corporate impressions?

4. One of the problems facing the agency's account team was selection of an appropriate tag line for its presentation, because a senior decision-making executive director in Frontier was particularly fond of the line, *The Joy of Light and Creativity*. What does an ad agency do when a particular individual in a client company expresses a desire for a particular tag line or image that the agency's account team believes from its own marketing analysis is inappropriate? What other kinds of constraints come into play during an agency's development of creative ideas for an advertising campaign? Is there any difference in attitudes towards creative work between copywriters and art directors working in Japan and those working in, say, the United States of America?

5. Preparations for the presentation to Frontier revealed several differences of opinion among members of the account and creative teams about how best to appeal to German and American consumers. In the end, one set of ads – the *Nature* series – was preferred by the Japanese staff, in spite of objections from the two foreigners present on the teams, suggesting that different peoples have different conceptions of how best to represent others. But were these likes and dislikes merely culturally based? Why does advertising make so much use of cultural stereotypes? Is there any difference in the ways that the Japanese represent 'the West', and those that 'Westerners' use to represent Japan?

6. This case study hinges on my own participation in ongoing events and the contribution that I was able to make, with a little help from my friends, to Asatsu's successful presentation to Frontier. This raises a methodological issue. What is the role of the participant observer in anthropological fieldwork? How much should he/she observe? How much should he/she participate? And how is one to blend the two? Are there any advantages to this kind of research in business organizations that other researchers might learn from? Isn't ethnographic fieldwork something that anyone going into business should practise as a matter of course in his or her everyday working life? Isn't a successful manager no less than a practising – and practised – fieldworker?

Part II
The Theories

–2–

Follow the Money

What does this case study have to tell us? As the final questions posed in the previous chapter intimate, the answer is: quite a lot of different things relating to different theoretical discussions, all stemming from the ethnographic material that you have just read. Thus one line of enquiry that I follow in the next chapter will look at how people talk about their work environment as a means towards understanding and 'narrating' corporate organization. Another will address the ways in which corporations interact with one another and make use of formalized ritualistic events to manage the impressions that they wish to foster on their partners and rivals. A third will discuss the headlines and visuals in the campaign prepared for Frontier by Asatsu and consider how 'creativity' is practised in an advertising agency, as well as the conditions that act as a constraining factor on such creative practices. Yet a fourth theoretical tack will look at how the images used in the Agency's campaign proposal reflect the ways in which a particular people constructs 'the other' in its collective imagination. For the moment, however, I want to concentrate on advertising accounts, the financial organization of the advertising industry and what this case study taught me to look for further during the remaining months of my fieldwork in Asatsu.

In the previous chapter, you will have noticed how the client company was already clearly well disposed towards Asatsu before handing over its account to the agency, and how closely agency and select client personnel interacted during the run-up to the presentation. The argument that I am going to present here is that such close interaction between agency and client is in large part attributable to the way in which the advertising account system operates in Japan. In other words, if we want to understand how the advertising industry works, we need to find out how money is circulated among the different players in that industry. Indeed, as a seasoned ethnographer who has in his time also studied folk art pottery, ceramic art exhibitions, whaling and fashion magazines, 'follow the money' is a good principle for anybody trying to find out about the organization and structure of *any* industry (and, indeed, about the whys and wherefores of particular government policies) anywhere in the world.

Advertising industries everywhere are structured around accounts – the sums of money put aside by advertisers and allocated to agencies for the purpose of selling a particular brand or product group, sometimes through a selected medium. But how do advertising clients distribute their accounts? How do they go about selecting one agency rather than another to work for them? What do accounts mean exactly to the men and women who work in an advertising agency? Why are they so important? And what are the organizational and other effects of their distribution both in the advertising industry as a whole and within particular agencies?

There are two reasons why any discussion of the structure and operation of any advertising industry in any part of the world must, strictly speaking, begin and end with its account system. In the first place, an agency's prosperity and profitability depend on its being able to successfully solicit and maintain accounts. This is no easy task. Although there are no hard and fast figures for Japan that I know of, in the United States it has been said that the average length of time for an account to stay with one agency is eight years.[1] In addition, 'Advertising agencies are service industries whose prosperity is totally determined by the prosperity of their clients, the advertisers.'[2] When clients have money to spend, agencies flourish; when they don't, they struggle.

Secondly, it is the distribution of accounts by companies wishing to advertise that permits full-service and specialized agencies, media organizations, production houses, and a host of other people (from freelance copywriters to stylists, by way of photographers, models and talent agencies) to contribute to the economy and culture of the advertising industry as a whole. In other words, accounts define the social world of advertising.

Accounts are competed for by different agencies, each of which tries to establish its worth or credibility with a client – what I shall later on discuss in greater detail under the heading of 'impression management'. On the one hand, such worth may be seen to lie in an agency's ability to liaise closely with the client during the handling of an account and it is account management that impresses a large body of advertisers. At the time of my research, Asatsu's forte was generally seen to be its ability to manage accounts in a very personal way that appealed to the agency's Japanese clients, in particular.

On the other hand, it may be an agency's brilliant display in positioning a client's product in the market, accompanied by an ability to create exciting visual ideas that perfectly express the results of the market research and analysis, which impresses the would-be advertiser and makes it value the agency's services. Indeed, it is its creative work that is sometimes seen as justification for a client's continued retention of a particular agency to handle its account, even when the advertiser feels that the agency concerned is not particularly adept at account management per se.

Periodically, however, whether it is in an account-management or creativity-based type of relationship,[3] a client will get tired of its agency and call for a competitive presentation, or what in the trade is often called a 'creative shoot-out' or 'gang bang'.[4] This is what happened when Asatsu was asked to compete with Frontier's contracted agency, J&M. As the case study made clear, shoot-outs are not the most efficient way for an advertising agency to spend its time or resources. Employees have to be taken away from other, ongoing tasks. They are asked to put in an enormous number of hours on a project that may very well not meet with success. And even when a presentation is successful, as was Asatsu's to Frontier, the new client does not necessarily accept the agency's campaign ideas, but asks it to start its preparations all over again (which is what actually happened with Frontier). Not surprisingly, therefore, shoot-outs have been described as 'carrot dangling on the grand scale, employed for the most part by unimaginative clients in the manner of a lame man grasping for a crutch'.[5]

Whether this is an appropriate description of Frontier's dealings with Asatsu I will leave to your judgement. The point I want to make here is that accounts do not just provide money to agencies to enable them to create advertising and so make money for themselves. More importantly, they define the organization of an advertising agency, as well as the structure of the advertising industry as a whole. For example, one of the things that became clear – if, at the time, but dimly so – during the course of my participation in preparations for the Frontier presentation was the importance of networks in the Japanese advertising industry.[6] It was the agency's ability to get behind the scenes and cultivate senior contacts in Frontier that was as crucial for its success in the shoot-out as anything else it did by way of creative campaign ideas. Unlike in many American or European agencies, too, copywriters and art directors were not expected to go around 'wearing their 'creativity' as a badge'.[7] Rather, it was a shared belief in teamwork that enabled the agency's account team to work together harmoniously, share ideas, and come up with marketing and creative solutions for the client's sales problem, and not some kind of more or less disguised notion of individual creative genius. Moreover, the fact that there were so many accounts being handled by Asatsu at any one time (600 was the going estimate) meant that account executives, market analysts, copywriters and art directors were working on all sorts of different accounts with all sorts of different people, thereby enabling a remarkable sharing of knowledge, information and networks within the agency. It is by examining how accounts are distributed in Japan's advertising industry, therefore, that I will show how the system of accounts affects both *inter*-organizational relations between advertising client, media organization and agency, on the one hand, and *intra*-organizational structure within an advertising agency, on the other.[8]

Competing and Split Accounts

In all advertising industries, the relationship between agency and client is a professional one in which much of the information exchanged is confidential (concerning, for instance, the launching of new products or the development of new marketing strategies). This means that clients tend to be very particular about which agency they select for what purpose – a concern that has given rise to the problem of what are known as competing accounts.

In the United States and Europe, as Yano and his colleagues emphasized time and time again during the course of my research, almost all companies refuse to allow their agencies to handle the advertising of products in direct competition with their own, and award the *whole* of their advertising account to a *single* agency which is not already contracted by a rival corporation.[9] As a result, no agency is able to handle the advertising accounts of both General Motors and Mercedes Benz; nor is it allowed to act on behalf of Unilever and Procter & Gamble, or Pepsi and Coca colas. If asked to take on a rival company's advertising account, therefore, an agency must decide whether to stick with its original client or not, and such factors as an account's size, prestige and growth potential, agency remuneration and client behaviour will affect that decision. Structurally speaking, the 'rule' about competing accounts ensures their continuous circulation by advertisers among different agencies, although just how stable an account is often depends on its size and the product category being handled.[10]

At the same time, however, we should note how broadly 'competition' might be (but generally is not) defined and that any agency will have difficulty in avoiding accounts that conflict if advertisers were to take into consideration not just their products, but, for example, price ranges, target audiences and use of materials (steel versus wood or plastics, for example). Thus, as Ralph Hower rightly points out: 'A policy of excluding all competing accounts from consideration, if *consistently* adhered to in *all* parts of the business, would so circumscribe efforts to get new clients that effective solicitation would be impossible' (italics added).[11]

The consistency argument is certainly one raised in the Japanese advertising industry, where – as every foreigner who has ever had dealings with Japanese advertising will be acutely aware – neither advertisers nor agencies are concerned about competing accounts.[12] Instead of handing over the whole of the advertising appropriation to a single agency, Japanese clients like Matsushita, Toyota and Shiseido split their accounts among a number of different agencies. Any agency, therefore, may in theory take on any Japanese advertiser's account, regardless of the fact that it may also be simultaneously contracted to carry out the advertising of a competing account, so that the split-account system not only overlooks, but actively encourages, competing accounts. As a result, agencies find themselves enmeshed in complicated sets of relationships which are, if not completely avoided, at least seemingly less intense in those advertising industries where the competing account rule holds good.

There are several ways by which the split-account system operates. Either, firstly, an advertiser splits its account according to *product ranges* (or *brands*), and contracts one agency to handle – say – its detergents, another its hair products, a third its soaps, and so on. Or, secondly, it splits its account by *media*, and contracts one agency to handle the television advertising of all its products, another newspaper (or print) advertising, a third radio, a fourth point of purchase advertising, a fifth promotional events, and so on.[13] Or, thirdly, it splits accounts according to *product and media*, contracting one agency to handle the television advertising, another the print advertising and a third the retail outlet promotions of, say, a particular model of car, while asking three other agencies to handle different media advertising campaigns for another of its models. A large Japanese agency like Dentsu or Hakuhodo, therefore, might be handling the Fuji and Tokyo (but not Asahi) channel television advertising for, say, Toyota's Corona; the outdoor advertising (excluding creative work) for its Corolla; buying space in the Yomiuri, Asahi and Mainichi newspapers on behalf of another agency contracted to do the creative work for the Corolla; and all print advertising (including creative work) for the Toyota Cedric.

Although a small handful of very large corporations in the United States and elsewhere have now adopted the first method above of splitting their advertising accounts by product ranges or brands, the major difference between their approach and that found in Japan is that all Japanese clients automatically accept the fact that their agencies may also be handling the accounts of rival corporations. When I was conducting my research in Asatsu, for example, the agency was – within my limited knowledge – handling several accounts split by both product and media of two Japanese car manufacturers (as well as the whole of a European motor corporation); four product lines put out by Japan Tobacco; and different aspects of the promotion and advertising of three airline companies, two banks, three breweries, two pharmaceutical and two life insurance firms, four major food and two household electrical appliance manufacturers. The only difficulty it faced with regard to its handling of these competing accounts was with its European motor corporation client.[14]

The question that arises from this is: how rational is the Japanese method of distributing advertising appropriations among numerous different agencies? Clearly, no business is ever completely rational. In Hower's nicely turned phrase: 'It is subject to the ever-present conflict of principles, the senseless whims of circumstance, and the idiosyncrasies of men.'[15] But there comes a point where those in business usually try to do something about the clash of non-logical and accidental, with rational, forces. If the split- account system indeed enmeshes those concerned in such complicated and undoubtedly irksome sets of binding relationships not found, or less prevalent, in other advertising industries, it is reasonable to ask why the Japanese continue with it. Could it be that there are some not immediately obvious, positive aspects to the difficulties that ensue from the handling of split accounts which help explain why the system continues to be used? Are these aspects such that advertising industries elsewhere might benefit from dropping the idea of competing accounts and adopting instead a split-account system?

The answers to this set of questions ultimately affect relations *between* agencies, their clients and media and other organizations of (Japan's) advertising industry, on the one hand, and the organization of personnel *within* (Japanese) advertising agencies (and, to some extent, within media organizations like newspapers, publishers and television stations), on the other. Although, as we shall see, it is somewhat artificial to set up a rigorous dichotomy between these two interdependent parts of the industry's structure and organization, I shall here treat them separately in order to make my argument clear.

Inter-Organizational Relations

The first and most important result of the split-account system is that it favours agencies in financial terms. Precisely because they *are* split, accounts are in general not nearly as large as those found in the United States. Moreover, there are far more accounts in circulation – as noted above, more than 600 in Asatsu – than is the case with an equivalent-sized American agency, which might be handling between just 40 and 50 accounts. Thus, when an agency loses an account, the financial implications of the loss are not such that its overall stability is threatened – in the way that it would be if it were operating in an industry where the competing account rule operates.[16] Of course, an agency may need to tighten its belt a notch or two, but it does not usually lay off employees when it loses a large account, since the sheer number of accounts in circulation means that it is likely to find a replacement account fairly promptly. In this respect, the split-account system indirectly supports what is known as the 'permanent employment' system found in major Japanese corporations and practised by most large agencies, and thus contributes to the overall stability of large organizations in particular within the industry.

At the same time, secondly, the split-account system is clearly a divide-and-rule mechanism which enables advertisers to operate a competitive lever with which to threaten, control and, as appropriate, reward (those working in) the agencies contracted. In other words, advertisers believe that, by dividing up their appropriations, they encourage keen competition among agencies which as a result (they hope) produce 'better' advertising (i.e. advertising that sells). The split-account system thus creates and sustains a system of hierarchical power relations between advertisers and agencies – in particular, with regard to manipulation of a variable commission system (see below).

This power structure between client and agency is further sustained, thirdly, by the fact that, because agencies are not asked to handle an entire campaign, they cannot readily know what is going on in other parts of their client's overall advertising and marketing strategy and thus do not have an overview of what is going on. This was why an account executive handling one of Frontier's domestic accounts in Asatsu was temporarily assigned to the international account team during its presentation preparations. He could provide Ueda with valuable information gleaned from both Frontier and media organizations about the client's overall sales and marketing strategies.

This situation partly deals with the problem of client confidentiality for which the competing account rule was established, in that the client retains effective control over information that it disseminates to its agencies. At the same time, however, it prevents an agency from carrying out the kind of *total* communication activities that it often claims to provide for would-be advertisers. How often would I hear account managers at Asatsu puzzling over how best to get access to client information that would help them in their marketing and creative strategies. It is this kind of unity in conception and execution of advertising campaigns that most agencies yearn for, but which is generally beyond their reach. It is this very lack of unity and conception that then allows mutual recrimination between client and agency, evasion of responsibility by both, and the resultant and continued circulation of accounts.

From this situation stem two organizational strategies. On the one hand, as I hinted above, in an attempt to gain information about other parts of an account on which it is working, an agency will liaise closely with media organizations. This it does, firstly, to find out how its own ideas compare with those being debated elsewhere (and passed on through media buyers asked to set up certain types of campaign with particular media organizations); and secondly, when taking on a new account, to find out what level of commission it can safely negotiate with its new client.[17] For example, by winning new accounts from the *same* client, an agency can learn that advertising rates are not necessarily as standard as media organizations would have it believe and that certain agencies get preferential treatment. This enables an agency to negotiate better rates for its media placement (rates that it may or may not pass on to clients). Moreover, by winning new accounts from *different* clients, an agency learns that media organizations also give *advertisers* special treatment. This encourages agencies to bargain harder and to play off one client in its portfolio against another. As a result, we find that extremely close contacts are maintained between agencies and media organizations in the Japanese advertising industry so that, together with their clients, they form what I have elsewhere referred to as the 'tripartite structure' of the industry.[18]

On the other hand, in an attempt to gain an ever larger slice of the advertising cake that it has already been given by a large, prestigious client, an agency will often agree to carry out low-level, less obviously visible (or rewarding) aspects of advertising and promotion, in the hope and expectation that it will eventually gain access to more lucrative, above-the-line contracts (particularly, of course, for television). For example, during my stay there, Asatsu carried out market questionnaires and analysis for a major computer firm in the belief that a job done well in this time- and personnel-consuming task would lead to its being asked to create and run a less labour-intensive and more profitable print advertising campaign. It also helped a large cosmetics company standardize its counters and point of purchase equipment at all retail outlets throughout the country in the hope that it might later be contracted to carry out media buying for in-house created advertising campaigns.[19] Thus the split-account system can be said to encourage every advertising agency to expand its activities into all aspects of Japan's consumer and other markets and in this way to allow it to refer to itself more honestly as a 'total communications' agency. In other words, Japanese agencies develop strong networks in all areas of the domestic economy and so sustain the concept of Japan as a 'network society'.[20]

Finally, and closely related to organizational networks within the Japanese advertising industry, I discovered from fieldwork that the split-account system encourages informal contacts between account executives working in an agency and their counterparts in client companies. Precisely because there *are* (more) slices of the advertising cake on offer, account executives in Japan spend a seemingly inordinate, and economically often unjustified, amount of time visiting advertising and product managers in (potential) client companies, and persuading them to offer their agency an opportunity to participate in a competitive presentation for a new account. In Asatsu, it was generally agreed that it is the personal relationship that develops between those concerned, rather than a more professional approach to planning and executing an account, that ultimately determines whether an account is awarded to and stays with a particular agency, is increased, decreased, multiplied or withdrawn.[21] In other words, the very number of accounts – and the competition that they generate among agencies, media, production companies and other organizations in the Japanese advertising industry – makes interpersonal relations an even more important factor in Japanese business relations than they already are in other advertising industries where the competing account system is found. This, too, supports Murakami and Rohlen's hypothesis that 'social exchange has diffused more significantly into the economic sphere in post-war Japanese society than in most other industrial societies.'[22]

Intra-organizational Relations

Let us now turn to ways in which the split-account system affects relations within an agency. As we have noted, accounts provide the sums of money that enable advertising and media organizations to function in the first place. Because they involve not just advertising itself, but sales strategies, corporate imaging, merchandising, media and other forms of promotion, accounts determine the functional units – (international) sales, marketing, media buying, promotions, creative, and so on – into which an agency is structured. At the same time, the broad nature of an account – involving at a minimum strategic planning, marketing analysis and creative ideas – makes cross-divisional co-operation essential within any agency.

This is not all. An agency deals with clients from all kinds of different businesses, each of which has its own organizational peculiarities (based in part on *their* business dealings in the particular industry of which they are part). It therefore needs to have an organizational structure that – unlike what is often suggested of other Japanese corporations[23] – displays maximum flexibility, since it must be able to adapt to the structure of each of its clients' business worlds. At the same time, this structure must be able to cope with the sheer number of accounts an agency handles on behalf of its different advertisers.

Whereas, in the United States or elsewhere where the competing account system exists, agencies tend to adopt *either* functional *or* accounts-based methods of organization,[24] Asatsu adopted both simultaneously. At the time of my research, there existed a hierarchical management structure of 10 offices, 23 divisions and 82 departments to house its 900 employees who handled over 600 accounts a year.[25] The minimum units of formal organization contained between five and ten persons who, in various combinations, handled as many as half a dozen, but more likely two or three, accounts – depending on their size and importance. They were generally led by those who had been successful with accounts (whether in their acquisition, development, analysis, creation, or whatever) and so helped Asatsu win more accounts from a client.

At the same time, this hierarchical organization was complemented by a 'flat' inter-departmental structure of account 'teams', consisting of all those in Asatsu working on a particular account at any one time. Usually, as the Frontier case illustrates, an account team was made up of at least one account executive, and small marketing and creative teams, with others being brought in from promotions, merchandising, and media buying as and when appropriate. It was the account team, led by the (senior) account executive, that thrashed out the (lack of) synergy effect between marketing analysis and creative ideas and that interacted with the client on a regular basis throughout the preparations leading up to the launch of its campaign.

By dividing employees into small 'groups' or 'rooms', as well as account 'teams', Asatsu was also able to obviate any potential problem of client conflict because it made sure that no single account services office (there were three in all at the time) handled more than one potentially competing account. Moreover, this division of the agency's organizational structure was maintained *spatially* by keeping different offices on different floors of its numerous different buildings and, in the case of account services (called 'sales', or *eigyō*, in Japanese), by not consolidating different departments within different divisions of the office as a whole. In this way, one car manufacturer's account was to be found on the eighth floor of one building near Shinbashi, a second on the fourth floor of the building next door and a third on the seventh floor of a building the far side of a major intersection down the road.

In this respect, the split-account system may be said to contribute to the effective functioning of an agency itself as an organization. For example, the creation of smaller, rather than overly large, offices and divisions facilitated the day-to-day and long-term strategic management of accounts and personnel. To ensure that managers were able to carry out their managerial functions properly and effectively, Asatsu's Board of Directors used to reshuffle accounts among the various divisions and departments according to the acquisition, loss, increase or decrease of accounts (whether new, old or existing) to ensure equitable and manageable distribution among them. This often led to the creation of new groups, departments, even divisions, and thus to the creation of new managerial positions for talented employees who had proved themselves in the field. The continual readjustment of the agency's organization as a result of the sheer number of split accounts circulating encouraged a strong sense of competitiveness among offices, divisions and departments, right down to individual employees.

In other words, the split-account system not only demands flexibility in an agency's organizational structure, but actively contributes to individual employees' promotion prospects. In this respect, it counters the malaise that has in the past affected many less flexibly organized corporations practising permanent employment and promotion by seniority in other industries within the Japanese economy. At the same time, the split-account system further supports the Japanese employment system in that the obvious opportunities for promotion encourage employees to remain with their agencies and not to shift to rival organizations or start up their own agencies (taking a favoured client with them), in the manner found in Western advertising industries. In short, as we saw previously in the relationship between split accounts, agency finance and permanent employment, Japanese advertisers' decision to divide up their appropriations contributes to the maintenance of a specifically Japanese form of what Ronald Dore has termed 'welfare capitalism'.[26]

Essentially 'Japanese'? Or with Global Potential?

In this chapter, I have taken the concept of account brought up in the Frontier case study and examined ways in which the split-account system influences both the structure of Japan's advertising industry and the internal organization of advertising agencies therein. From this it is possible to embark upon two interrelated, but rather different, strands of discussion. One concerns the contribution of the split-account system to the maintenance of a specifically 'Japanese' advertising industry; the other the possibility of its adoption in advertising industries elsewhere in the world.

Let me start with the first of these strands. I have argued that the split-account system encourages advertising agencies to expand into below-the-line promotional activities – activities that they might otherwise leave to specialist houses – in the hope that these will persuade their clients to reward them with more lucrative and less labour-intensive above-the-line accounts. In other words, agencies are obliged to provide the fullest of 'full services' if they are to survive and grow. As a result, they find themselves working as jacks-of-all-trades, arranging the annual sales convention of a major automobile manufacturer, on the one hand, and devising – and then running – a large brewery's centenary celebrations that are then transformed into a major direct-marketing effort, on the other.[27] Among other things, they also arrange performances of Italian opera, dream up television programmes, market associated merchandise, carry out the total corporate identity transformation of an airline company (including redesigning the interiors of all its planes), propose new venues for advertising (from telegraph poles and tram tickets in the early days of Japanese advertising to video boards and boarding passes now), and act as go-betweens in celebrity marriages. In this way, they can properly describe themselves as providers of 'total intelligence communications'.

I have also shown how the system of splitting accounts by Japanese advertisers helps sustain a 'Japanese' style of market capitalism by indirectly supporting the kind of 'permanent' employment structure found in large firms in Japan. In this respect, precisely because of its comparative 'uniqueness' (which presents a problem of immediate comprehensibility), the split-account system obliges the localization of global business strategies and so contributes to the overall myth that the Japanese market is somehow 'different' from markets elsewhere. It may thus be a ploy to *protect* the Japanese advertising industry from the kind of invasion by foreign – that is, primarily American – agencies that has occurred in almost all other countries in the world. After all, what other advertising industry outside of the United States is able to boast that it has not a single foreign name among its top ten agencies?

There is, however, another aspect of the relation between the split-account system and the 'Japaneseness' of the advertising industry that should be noted here. For a long time now, differences in employment structures, inter-company mobility, separation of corporate ownership from management, decision-making styles, working hours, employees' background education, salary levels, and so on have been noted in discussions of large and small businesses in Japan.[28] This has led to the definition of what Rodney Clark has referred to as a 'status gradation of industry', whereby Japanese businesses are ranked in a number of different streams (*ryū*) in a prestige system related to their overall success, size, profitability, and so on.[29] Not only the companies themselves, but people everywhere – from employees to consumers – are very aware of the accumulation of economic and cultural capital[30] by companies and are, as a result, actively interested in these rankings which also, of course, apply to the organization of the Japanese advertising industry. Not only are advertisers, agencies and media organizations all ranked in economic terms according to their successes and failures within their own spheres of business; they gain and lose social prestige from the business associations that they enter into with one another.

It is in this context that the split-account system takes on considerable significance. Accounts are not simply sums of money. Like art objects, they bring with them certain values that are not purely economic, but derive from their ownership (or provenance), history and association (with previous agencies, for example). In advertising industries all over the world, therefore, agencies gain prestige from the clients whose accounts they are contracted to handle. (Such cultural capital is overtly recognized in the Anglo-American advertising world by the term 'blue chip'.) Just how such prestige is circulated, therefore, becomes very important. In a system of competing accounts, for example, there are only so many blue-chip accounts to go round and the prestige attached to them has the same effect as their financial magnitude. In other words, the rise and fall of an agency's cultural capital accompanying the win and loss of a major account of a blue-chip client can be precipitous.

In an advertising industry where accounts are split, however, there are clearly far more blue-chip accounts in circulation (even though they may be of less financial value). That is, there are more opportunities for agencies to build up cultural, as opposed to simply economic, capital because several different agencies can associate themselves symbolically with major corporate names like Mitsubishi, Sumitomo, Matsushita, Shiseido and Mitsui. In this way, they have readier access than agencies functioning in a competing account system to a portfolio of accounts that contributes to and sustains their own overall position within the industry's prestige hierarchy. In this respect, therefore, the split- account system clearly contributes both to the status gradation of the Japanese advertising industry, as well as to a specifically 'Japanese' aspect of the domestic economy as a whole.

Perhaps I should add a coda to this discussion of economy and culture. This relates to the distinction made between creative- and account-driven advertising.[31] It is clear that, as a general rule, American and European advertising agencies pride themselves on their 'creativity' (however such a word may be defined) and it is such creativity that is used, firstly, to persuade would-be advertisers that one particular agency is 'better' than another and, secondly, to sell whatever is being advertised. In Japan, however, although some agency managers may from time to time bemoan the fact, creativity is seen to be of far less importance. Not only is there virtually no major Japanese agency CEO who is a copywriter or art director by trade, the hierarchical divisional structure of most agencies places the sales (or account services) division 'above' the creative division, and emphasizes the fact that the former is a 'profit' and the latter a 'cost' centre.

Why the difference between the two? The answer is by no means clear-cut. Although I shall return to discuss constraints on creativity in a later chapter, an argument can, I think, be made here in terms of the relation between economic and cultural capital and the type of account system that drives that relation.[32] Where accounts are split, as in Japan, agencies find themselves working much more closely with clients in their everyday lives. As a result, they tend not to be given anything like a free rein in the preparation of advertising campaigns and an agency's focus tends to be on the account itself (that is, on the prevailing relations between agency and client), rather than on the product of an account (the advertising produced by its creative staff in co-operation with account planners, market analysts and media buyers). In other words, it is account management, rather than creativity, that is the focus of an agency's attention.

This tends not to be the case in countries where the competing account rule prevails although, historically, the industry tends to swing between the two poles of creativity and account management, as we shall see. Having awarded an account, a client tends not to interfere in the everyday affairs of the agency contracted to prepare its advertising campaign. Here lies the rub. While Japanese agencies find themselves engaged in constant (re)negotiation with their clients over the work they are contracted to do, European and American agencies are allowed to work in comparative isolation from their clients. As a result, the latter have over the years developed – like many institutions concerned with cultural production – an ethos that represses the narrowly economic or commercial interest of advertising in what amounts to 'collective misrecognition' (in Bourdieu's phrase). Instead, they have taken advantage of the freedom given them by the system of competing accounts to 'create' a myth of 'creativity' that is used to set themselves apart from their rivals, as well as on an equal, preferably higher, pedestal than that occupied by their clients.[33] Creativity thus becomes the source of an agency's cultural capital and is used in part as an ideological tool to offset its clients' economic power. In short, the system of competing accounts has permitted European and American advertising agencies to assert symbolic independence from the financial power of the clients upon whom they depend for their economic existence, and to make use of their cultural capital (that is, creativity) to transform that power into their own economic capital (by winning accounts).

This is an issue, as I mentioned, that we shall return to in Chapter 5, but it brings us nicely to the second part of the discussion. Earlier on in this chapter, I hinted that perhaps the split-account system served some important business and social functions within the Japanese advertising industry, in spite of all appearances to the contrary to those of us not familiar with its operations. In particular, I asked – partly as devil's advocate – whether it might be possible that advertising industries in Europe and the United States would be better served by adopting a split, rather than competing, account system. At the time, I suspect, anyone already conversant with the way advertising works thought the idea preposterous. While mindful of the often opposing views adopted by those participating in the advertising industry, let me now sum up what I see as the pros and cons of the method of Japanese advertisers' dividing their appropriations among two or more agencies.

1. The split-account system clearly keeps the advertising industry as a whole internally stable.[34] This is to everyone's advantage. Of course, booms and depressions in the economy as a whole affect the amounts put aside for advertising by Japanese corporations. But, within the industry as a whole, the splitting of accounts helps keep all agencies, and thus all the subsidiary or dependent firms that rely on agencies' advertising, promotional and sales campaigns, in a fairly stable financial situation. As I pointed out, the loss of a single account – however large – is not likely to upset the overall equilibrium of an advertising agency, unless it is very small. There are thus important *financial* effects of the split-account system that make it preferable to the system of competing accounts.

2. Advertisers in Japan know that they can always choose the agency that they like the best (for whatever reason or reasons). Elsewhere, it is an agency's decision as to whether it will or will not accept or ditch an account. In other words, the awarding of accounts in Japan is in the hands of the advertisers whereas, where the competing account rule prevails, agencies decide whether to accept or refuse an account. Here, and in the following two paragraphs, we are concerned with issues of *power and control*.

3. So far as advertisers themselves are concerned, the split-account system sustains their control over agencies that cannot get ready access to the entirety of their clients' marketing, sales and promotional strategies. To overcome what they see as the weak point of the system (that they are not given an overall vision enabling them to create a really special campaign), agencies find themselves more or less forced to network with other agencies and media organizations and thus to get information that is not readily or directly available from their clients. As a result, the split-account system both creates and sustains a power hierarchy between advertisers and agencies, on the one hand, and – as a means of offsetting that power – encourages interdependence among all those participating in the advertising industry, on the other.

4. Precisely because agencies want to gain access to other parts of their clients' accounts, they initiate all kinds of marketing and promotional strategies outside the confines of above-the-line advertising. This enables them to broaden their knowledge base and to use that knowledge strategically to their advantage in dealings with new and existing clients, thereby helping them become full service agencies. In this respect, advertising agencies in Japan tend to take on a multi-functional role that might be distributed among different organizations (such as marketing analysts, consultants, and so on) in industries where the

competing account rule prevails. Agencies become the lynchpin of the industry, and the focus of responsibility, including failure and success (although clients tend, as elsewhere, to take credit for the latter).

5. Finally, and here the issue is one of internal management control and corporate *organization*, the sheer variety of tasks taken on by an agency as a result of the split-account system encourages an organizational structure that is extremely flexible. As I have shown, a number of things – including, for example, competitiveness and promotion opportunities – follow from this need for an agency to function effectively in business situations. At the same time, the fact that agencies are structured both hierarchically in divisions (by whatever name) and horizontally by means of hundreds of cross-divisional account teams means that there is considerable cross-over by individual employees into different areas of an agency's business and corporate structure. As a result, they learn a lot about their organization and interact a lot with colleagues in other areas of business conducted by their agency. This in itself leads to a stronger sense of corporate belonging and unity than would otherwise be the case.

–3–

Advertising Talk

One of the things I quickly learned – and doubtless you will have noticed – from the Frontier account presentation was that making ads is mainly a matter of talk. Meetings of all kinds (account team, departmental, agency-client and follow-up post-mortem, shareholders, press, plus endless others);[1] surveys, questionnaires, interviews, focus groups, market analyses, positioning statements; brand workshops,[2] product and brand recommendations, creative strategy and communication; presentations, speeches, greetings, congratulations and commiserations; instructions, advice, and warnings; stories, telephone calls, corridor gossip, lunch breaks, drinking sessions and rounds of golf; TV commercial production, studio photography, cast assembly, fashion and styling, sound recording, and everything else that could be conceivably involved in the creation of an advertising campaign – they all revolved around talk. And it was through talk that the everyday business of Asatsu was accomplished.[3]

And as I worked with my colleagues on preparations for the agency's presentation to Frontier, we talked: about Frontier, about the client's various accounts, about rival agencies, and about all the people and institutions (corporate clients, publishing houses, television networks, production shops, celebrities, and so on) that made up the field or world of Japanese advertising. But my colleagues also talked about their own advertising agency: about the people who worked there; the jobs that they did; and the who-did-what-when-why-and-with-what-result kind of talk that often takes the form of gossip. In the end, they even talked about my own contribution to what had become a successful presentation.

My interest in talk makes sense on at least two counts. Firstly, I am an anthropologist, and my classical Greek education reminds me that the word anthropologist literally means someone who listens to talk about people and then talks about people,[4] and that what an anthropologist studies is 'how people in other communities construct their world by conversing about it'.[5] Secondly, talk is carried on by people, and organizations are themselves people[6] – a point well understood by senior management in the agency who frequently used to stress that 'Asatsu is people'. It is the talk that I heard and myself participated in that has structured my understanding and account of Asatsu. It is through talk that those working for Asatsu engaged with their organization's structural constraints, at the same time as actively structuring, or 'enacting', both the agency and, through it, the field of advertising in which it was positioned and positioned itself by means of ongoing accounts and advertising campaigns.

The talk that I record here is primarily – though by no means exclusively – that between my 'informants' and myself. The fieldwork fragments of talk gathered in this way often coalesced into stories, and stories – both those that people told me and told among themselves – can teach the ethnographer 'a great deal about the structure and culture of an organization'.[7] Not only is storytelling 'the institutional memory system of the organization'.[8] At the heart of all storytelling is the imparting of something useful to the listener – whether a moral, practical advice or a maxim.[9] In Asatsu, stories were used to transform information into first-hand experience and it was those already with such experience who told the stories in order to enable their listeners (new recruits, comparative newcomers and myself as fieldworker) to get a feel for what it meant to be working in the advertising industry.[10]

But the way in which I record talk and accompanying stories also reflects my own craft of telling stories. The joint performance of both storyteller and listener that characterizes a story[11] is thus carried over from face-to-face oral communication to a written text in which a new audience (of readers) engages with a new storyteller (the author) in a new joint performance of that same story. In other words, the writing of stories is itself a story of writing, in which, as author, I choose to select certain themes, on the basis of perceived relevance and importance, and ignore others. This choice then results in the structure of this book.

The Frontier case study exemplifies this communicative situation very well since the account team's success provided agency employees with a story that directly affected my own research. Word of my participation in the competitive presentation obviously got around very quickly. Before the end of the week, two or three senior account managers with whom I had previously had only a nodding acquaintance stopped me in corridors or elevators to comment on and thank me for my contribution. At the same time, others began to approach me out of the blue to ask me for suggestions about presentation or campaign ideas that they were working on. Could I comment on a creative brief for All Nippon Airlines' new business class travel arrangements? Could I think of a headline to harness a fabric softener to a particular target market? Could I advise a senior account executive on the potential problems arising out of a joint venture with a Russian business partner? And so on. In this respect, talk about my participation in and contribution to a successful presentation encouraged a number of employees to enter into strategic exchange networks with me. I say 'strategic exchanges'[12] because, while I provided them with various ideas and pieces of advice (hopefully, not always taken up), they provided me with a much fuller and more rounded picture of the agency's activities and thus with a more coherent understanding of the field of advertising as a whole.

In terms of the more specialized work in which advertising practitioners themselves engaged, this chapter contains a number of different sorts of talk about products, people and organizations of one sort or another. On the one hand, it recounts how an advertising agency in a way advertises itself – both to its employees and to people with whom it has business dealings of one sort or another in the outside world. This advertising of advertising practices is something that I shall take up again, albeit in a different theoretical context, in the following chapter, but for the moment just let us note that an advertising agency is in many respects a storytelling organization on two counts. Firstly, its employees use talk and stories to explain their own actions, as well as those of their colleagues in the work community, in order to give shape to that community, and create and negotiate the multiple meanings that sustain it. Such talk and stories also provide them with practical experiences on which to base their own actions during everyday business interaction with other members of the advertising industry. Secondly, agency members talk and tell stories about products and organizations through the advertising campaigns that they create for their clients.

On the other hand, this chapter is a tale of how different people in Asatsu perceived ongoing and past events in different but related ways and talked about them to one another, as well as to myself. As such, it describes the structuring processes of an organization through its everyday forms of communication.[13] Not surprisingly, perhaps, I soon discovered that the Frontier case study provided a number of stories that I later understood were woven into several different ongoing discourses of talk about Asatsu, the world of advertising and Japanese business methods. Moreover, as I gradually began to put together my understanding of what it was like to work in a large Japanese advertising agency, I realized that agency talk tended to converge around three main themes:

1. The history of the advertising agency as an emergent corporation in Japan's advertising industry (what I shall here call *Tales of the Past*).[14]
2. Networking and the sharing of information and gossip as part of the agency employees' everyday work routines (*Tales of the Now*).
3. Use of both *Tales of the Past* and *Tales of the Now* as part of the agency's ongoing strategic planning with regard to accounts – the sums of money paid to agencies by advertisers to enable them to plan, create and market advertising campaigns (*Tales of Reproduction*).

It is these three slightly different, but frequently overlapping sets of tales that I shall try to relate now.

Tales of the Past

Referring as they do to events that have come to an end, *Tales of the Past* are incorporated into organizational history and folklore. Asatsu's history, as related here, was very much a part of the talk that those employed would engage in when confronted by an inquisitive newspaper reporter or visiting anthropologist. In summary form it was written down and presented on slides to potential clients who had asked the agency to prepare an advertising campaign presentation (often in competition with other agencies). A slightly more detailed history was printed in the *Handbook* that the agency provided for all its new recruits at the beginning of every April. This listed the agency's most famous success stories – its breakthrough into television advertising through the marketing of animation films, the winning of a major blue-chip account and the introduction of its marketing computer system, for example. It also talked of its own contributions and adaptations to the advertising industry in which it operated: pre-paid postcards first inserted in magazines in 1956; the introduction of magazine contents page advertising in 1959; the transformation of a comic strip into an animated film in 1963; the adoption of the creative director system in 1970; and so on. The *Handbook* also tied the agency's achievements into the broader context of the post-war growth of the Japanese economy, as well as of the advertising and media world in which the agency operated.

Talk of the past was by no means all written down, however, and members of Asatsu who had been there for twenty, thirty, even forty years liked to reminisce about how the agency used to be and what it was that drove it ever onward to its present success. In general, this kind of talk focused on three complementary themes.

Firstly, it extolled the charismatic virtues of the founding CEO and present Chairman of the Agency, Masao Inagaki, who in spite of his advancing age (he was at the time in his late sixties) was still actively involved in the strategic planning of the agency's business. Inagaki was widely respected not only by his employees (who eagerly used to recount how he had memorized details about their private lives), but also by those working in the advertising industry as a whole.

> My marriage was arranged by the CEO. That's something he's done quite a lot for other Asatsu employees – acting as go-between. And yet he still remembers all sorts of personal details about my wife and me – our dates of birth, which schools and universities we went to, our wedding anniversary, and so on. I really respect him for that.

Inagaki was regarded as being 'human',[15] and a Japanese businessman of the best possible kind – combining intellectual acumen, tough negotiating practice and an ethical integrity that are virtually unmatched among his peers. Talk about the CEO thus emphasized his personality, energy and strategic vision, as well as his unassuming attitude of mild compliance (*sunaosa*) – qualities that were, it was made clear by those talking about him, absolutely essential prerequisites for any advertising executive who wished to make a success of his or her career.

> The CEO's a remarkable man. You've already heard him lecture you with great energy and enthusiasm this morning. You've had a chance to appreciate the kind of tactical skills he's used over the years to make Asatsu into such a successful advertising agency. And yet he doesn't put on airs at all. He's *sunao*. These are the kinds of qualities you yourselves need to cultivate as new employees in Asatsu. Practise them at all times. It is being *sunao* that'll set you apart, in the end, from advertising executives in other agencies like Dentsu and Hakuhodo.

> I first came to Asatsu to tell the Personnel people I was *not* going to accept the job they'd offered me, but was going to join another agency instead. But when I got here, the office was as busy as a bee's nest, with people coming and going all over the place, and I thought how exciting the agency looked. And then the CEO came into the room where I was sitting and said a few words to me. He was so unassuming. I mean, he basically asked me to come and work for him. So I ended up telling the *other* agency that I wasn't going to work for it. Asatsu was really dynamic.

In other words, by *not* setting Inagaki up as 'god',[16] this type of story of the past provided those working in the Agency with a sense of corporate identity and organizational philosophy. *Tales of the Past* contained all the manifestations of the leader-follower relation noted by Yiannis Gabriel: idealization, identification with leader, identification with other followers, suspension of most critical faculties and an uplifting quality.[17] They provided employees with a sense of what it meant to be an 'Asatsu-man' and so linked personal and organizational identity.[18] This was the gist of stories told about why people had come to, and remained working in, Asatsu:

> I was interested in advertising when I was at university, but when I tried to get a job I quickly found myself in trouble. Nobody wanted me because I was a woman university graduate. Asatsu was the only agency prepared to hire me. That's why I came here. And I guess that's why I'm still here.

> When I started out, I wanted to be a copywriter. But instead I was put into account services because, apparently, there weren't enough people to carry out the necessary tasks there. So I very reluctantly did what was asked of me, even though I spent most of the time asking myself why I was doing such a horrible job when all I wanted to do was be a copywriter. After a year, therefore, I went to the CEO and asked him to release me from being an account executive. He said: 'Oh dear. Do you really want to be a copywriter? I'm so sorry. But it will, of course, be very difficult for those you leave behind in account services. Don't you think you could stick it out for a little longer? You see, if you leave, the others will be in a real mess.'
>
> So I found myself doing a second year in a job I hated, and at the end of it I went back to Inagaki who said: 'Oh dear. Do you really dislike being an account executive

so much? And just when you're getting so good at it. Why don't you do just one more year in account services? By the end you'll have mastered your job, and you can then move on to copywriting.'

So I stuck it out for another year. And it was during that year that I suddenly appreciated the joy of working as an account executive. And now I've been doing the same job for the last 29 years. I never became a copywriter, after all.

Secondly, and as practical support to the above, those in senior and middle management positions often recounted cases of the Agency's successes (and occasional failures) in the advertising business. Here talk would stress, for example, a junior account executive's perseverance against all odds;[19] an account planner's ability to come up with a 'Big Idea'[20] (like repositioning a Polaroid camera as a visual stationery item, or introducing the concept of a 'morning shower' that altered everyday social behaviour in Japan); or even the beads of perspiration that visibly transformed an account executive's face as he 'gave his all' (*isshō kenmeisa*) during an important presentation to a blue-chip client (as Tanaka noted of Ueda during the latter's pitch for the Frontier account).

Sometimes, such tales were told to provide background to ongoing events – like when a prestigious European car manufacturer decided to review its account with Asatsu and called for a competitive presentation (something to which we will return later on in this chapter).

We were really quick off the mark. Back in the summer of 1986, somebody noticed a small newspaper article reporting that PKW, which had previously been selling its cars through the major dealer Yanase, was going to set up its own subsidiary company. We found out who the president of the subsidiary was going to be and used our networks to approach him.

We'd had plenty of experience in handling the Toyobishi car account, of course, and that helped immensely. But we weren't used to the luxury end of the car market. And we had very little experience of foreign clients. So we conducted a really expensive survey to find out as much as we could. It was these two things that put us in a good position when PKW invited us to participate in a competitive presentation the following February.

Asatsu devoted a lot of energy, manpower and money to winning that account. The CEO pulled out all the stops on that one, and no expense was spared. Well, there was one exception. In those days, the agency was housed in the old Shin'ichi Building where the men's and women's toilets faced the elevators on each floor. Somebody realised they wouldn't make a very good impression on our European visitors as they stepped out of the lift to go to the presentation, so enquiries were made about hiring a gold screen to be placed in the elevator lobby for the day. When it was learned this would cost $2,000 an hour, the CEO put his foot down. He wasn't going to pay so much for so little. So the agency's employees formed a human screen, with everybody lined up along the wall opposite the lift from which the PKW people emerged. That way the presence of the toilets was hidden. And Asatsu's manpower really impressed the client.

Nobody knows what really happened – apart from a very few people at the top, of course. But anyway, Asatsu won the account. They say it was partly the know-how the agency had developed with the Toyobishi account. But it seems like the fact that nobody in Asatsu really spoke fluent English, and yet still managed to get their ideas across, also had an influence on PKW's decision. They were impressed by our ability to communicate our own ideas – unlike Dentsu, which brought in fluent English speakers to present other people's work and creative ideas.

When Asatsu won the PKW account, the CEO had to buy two cars from the client. And he didn't even get a discount. The two agencies which lost the presentation, though, were each given a PKW car! I don't think Inagaki has ever used either of the PKW cars, though. He's got a perfectly good chauffeur-driven Toyobishi to commute to work in.

Such talk of the past was designed to support by actual examples the philosophical principles underpinning Asatsu's organization, and served to remind all concerned of the qualities expected of them as employees, as well as of the CEO's loyalty to established clients. At the same time, this particular tale of the past grappled with another ongoing problem: how to deal with foreign clients and get them to accept that the Japanese market and Japanese business methods were 'different'.

In general, however, *Tales of the Past* stressed principles generally seen to be characteristic of Japanese corporate organization: hard work, perseverance, trust, doing one's best, working together and long-term relationships, although Asatsu employees were also expected to use their initiative, creativity and individual judgement as appropriate. To take just two more examples:

There was a prestigious account we were trying to win. And it all seemed to boil down to account management. So I was detailed to get behind the scenes and find out as much as I could about the client. One day I managed to get an appointment with the sales manager there, and when I went into his office I spotted a rival agency's presentation plan on his desk. As I talked to him, I kept glancing down and trying to read upside down the one page executive summary of that agency's proposal. I think I must have got most of it right because the AE in charge of our account used what I told him to reposition our own presentation, and we won the account.[21]

When the Unicharm account was still very small, one account executive went time and time again to the client's office with proposals of all sorts, giving suggestions about how the client might want to market one of its products one day, or support an event another day, and so on. Eventually he met with success and the account is now one of our bigger ones. This is a good example of the kind of attitude an account executive needs to have. You can go to a company 30 times and be totally ignored. After your 40th visit, those concerned might secretly decide to award you some business once you've been there 50 times. And then you unwittingly spoil it all by giving up in despair after the 48th or 49th visit.

Thirdly, throughout the decades during which he was CEO of Asatsu, Inagaki developed his own management philosophy. This included an emphasis on learning (in order to enable his employees to come up with creative ideas), on personality (since advertising success depends very much on good personal interrelations), and on individual judgement. With regard to the last he promulgated a particular attitude towards his subordinates' decision-making processes that flew in the face of virtually everything that has ever been written about 'Japanese management style'. Rather than insist on business-related matters being referred back to management for authorization of action, Inagaki advocated what he called a 'total management system' (*zen'in keieishugi*), which permitted any employee at any level to take decisions while negotiating with clients.

> The other day, I was having lunch with PKW's sales manager when he asked me whether I could take over the account from the present account manager who he hasn't been getting on well with. I had to make a snap decision. So I promised to do so, in spite of all the other work I've got on my plate, because I knew it might make a difference to the client. I could do this without consulting my divisional boss because of the CEO's philosophy of total management.

In this respect, as CEO, Inagaki managed to overcome the formidable challenge facing all visionary leaders who need to: 'Offer a story, and an embodiment, that builds on the most credible of past syntheses, revisits them in the light of present concerns, leaves open a space for future events, and allows individual contributions by the persons in the group'.[22]

The fact that even the most junior employee could, in theory, make a decision instantly without having to worry (too much) about what his immediate department head or divisional chief might have to say about it, was often used in *Tales of the Past* to 'explain' Asatsu's historical success. Without such a rapid decision-making process, it was said, the agency would never have been able to win certain accounts or to make such headway in the advertising world. Only with this kind of decision-making process were employees allowed to develop and give full rein to their individual judgement.

Although 'total management' was generally mentioned in positive contexts like this, there was the very occasional oblique criticism that emerged, usually in a time of crisis:

> Total management has its down side, too, even though it's been the driving force behind Asatsu's success during the time I've been here. I mean, if a guy *does* make a wrong decision that jeopardises agency-client relations, like Mr Automobile did with PKW,

top management can't take him off the account totally. That would go against the CEO's philosophy of total management. So we end up having to make do with half measures – like shift him from above-the-line to below-the-line activities – and hope for the best.

Generally speaking, therefore, *Tales of the Past* were used to link organizational philosophy with corporate practices, on the one hand, and to provide bearings for employees as Asatsu continued its journey into uncharted territories in the advertising world, on the other. In serving these two overall purposes they had three important aims:

1. They helped employees differentiate Asatsu from other advertising agencies. In this respect, *Tales of the Past* were concerned with the creation of an overall corporate culture and thus with *corporate branding*.[23]
2. They incorporated Asatsu into a 'family' of major Japanese corporations that practised particularly 'Japanese' styles of (lifetime) employment and 'Confucian' management practices (including an emphasis on learning). At the same time, they were used to distinguish Asatsu from such corporations since the agency did *not* strictly adhere to seniority promotion; nor did its employees form an (enterprise) union.
3. They promulgated the Agency's business practices as the 'best' and most 'ethical' in the Japanese advertising industry. This was a necessary element in this kind of talk because advertising relies to a very large extent upon interpersonal relations among people employed in agencies, clients and media organizations, and because advertising people can as a result become involved in such questionable practices as bribery, corporate blackmail, and the 'doctoring' of media information.

Tales of the Now

Tales of the Now focused on emergent, unfolding events in the everyday working lives of agency employees. They aimed, firstly, to disseminate information that could be acted upon (and thus made into experience) *within* the agency. Such talk emerged in the form of ongoing projects, problems, strategic issues and the lessons to be learned from what was currently going on in the advertising world. Some of it took place in all the different kinds of formal meetings in which agency personnel participated – from the CEO's monthly address,[24] to the Media Buying Division's weekly update on unfilled advertising slots in print and broadcast media. A lot more occurred as employees from different divisions of the agency (account planning, marketing, creative, promotions, international, media buying, SP and so on) shared information, relayed gossip and rumour, and maintained carefully massaged networks of contacts in the advertising, media and entertainment worlds, as well as among (potential) clients. Here *Tales of the Now* focused very much on day-to-day events and were used as an integral part of the agency's strategic positioning vis-à-vis both (potential) advertising clients and the media organizations with which it worked. Take, for example, the unfolding of the following fragments of talk that together constitute an intricate story with plot involving four main characters and all sorts of potential sub-plots:

Have you heard the latest? You know Katsu Shintarō, the actor who plays the blind swordsman Zatoichi? Well, he's just been arrested in Honolulu airport for possession of 1.75 grams of cocaine and 9.75 grams of marijuana hidden away in his underwear. He paid a $1,000 fine and he's expected to be deported from Hawaii in a few days' time.

The thing is, Katsu's just completed a series of TV commercials for Kirin Beer – a series that was due to be aired throughout the year in a major campaign designed to help the company rake back some of the market share that it lost in the wake of Asahi's launching of its *Super Dry* beer. Katsu was seen to be the celebrity best suited to Kirin's marketing riposte of *nama* – 'raw' or 'live' – draught lager because his performances as the blind swordsman were invariably energetic and 'raw'. Six different commercials have already been completed and the first was shown on TV only two days ago. But Kirin's now cancelled the whole campaign because it's afraid viewers will react negatively if the brewer continues to use a celebrity who's been found guilty of possession.

The first newspaper ad went out a couple of weeks ago and Kirin had already booked space in all four main media – all through Hakuhodo which stood to make a lot of money from handling the year-long campaign. But now the whole thing's cancelled. The question is: who's going to pay for the six commercials already finished?

Those commercials cost several hundred million yen, you know. What's worse, they weren't one-offs, but were designed to follow one another and make a dramatic story. Hakuhodo was the agency involved and it persuaded Kirin to spare no expense. So a famous scriptwriter was hired for the campaign, as were several well-known actors and actresses. A lo-ot of money.

I heard Hakuhodo really pushed the idea of using Katsu in the Kirin commercials, even though some people inside Kirin thought this might be risky, given Katsu's past record. He's been questioned before, you know, though not charged.

The thing is, an agency is usually responsible for all expenses incurred during production of a campaign – payment of actors, cameramen, studio sets, sound, stylists, and so on. It also has to pay the media in cash once it places an ad or commercial, and it is only later that the client will pay both media charges and expenses. It's then that the agency can take its percentage and make a profit. Even so, hardly any clients – banks and financial institutions are welcome exceptions – actually pay *cash*. Instead, they send a credit note that can only be redeemed for cash after 90 days. What precisely's going to happen in this case is hard to tell. I somehow doubt agency-client relations will be completely severed, even though Kirin may be understandably annoyed at Hakuhodo's misjudgement of Katsu. Still, a new TV campaign has to be worked on now and it may be that Kirin will ask another agency to handle the draught lager account. It's just possible, too, that we may get asked to help. After all, we have an account with Kirin, though it's for another product. But one thing I tell you we won't do is: we won't approach Kirin and offer to help, just because Hakuhodo's made a mess of things. That would be in very bad taste.

In all probability, Hakuhodo signed a contract for the campaign with Kirin Beer and Katsu Promotions, the production company owned by the actor. And in this contract there should be a clause covering this sort of problem, where a celebrity for one reason or another fails to behave in an appropriate manner. The trouble is, along with Takakura Ken and Mifune Toshiro, Katsu is known as one of the 'three crows' (*samba karasu*) of the celebrity world. In other words, he's really difficult. Which means there's no knowing what parts of the contract Hakuhodo may have shelved in its attempt to secure Katsu's agreement to appear in the Kirin campaign.

The problem isn't really one of Hakuhodo's standing to lose $6 million, the way the newspapers presented it this morning. Kirin has something like 70 per cent of the Japanese lager market. That comes to about $7–8 billion a year. But it might lose something like $100 million in revenues because of this Katsu drug business. Given that its own annual billings are in the region of $5 billion, Hakuhodo won't even consider the financial implications of what's happened yet. Rather, they'll move rapidly into damage control mode. So far as the agency's concerned, a train has merely been derailed. What it needs to do, therefore, is send out a task force to mend the track and send the express on its way again. That's the way Hakuhodo sees things right now. After all, Kirin Beer is a very big account.

As for Kirin, it'll sit tight and say nothing. It'll watch how Hakuhodo reacts to the whole situation, and it may be a month or two before anything's said, or negotiations are begun. So it is *how* Hakuhodo behaves now that's of real interest. Funnily enough, if things go well, the agency may actually be able to *in*crease its stock with the client, rather than lose the account as some people anticipate. You never can tell. That's the way the advertising business is. But I can tell you *we* aren't going to do anything … We're comparatively small fry and it's highly unlikely Kirin would ask us to take over from Hakuhodo. So there's no way I'm going to start preparing a speculative presentation, or anything like that. To tell you the truth, I'm uneasy about what's happened, if only because our own business depends on the prosperity of our clients. If Kirin's sales go down – and it'll take a couple of months before we know for sure how consumers and retailers are reacting to the Katsu business – then Asatsu will suffer, too. So I don't feel like thumbing my nose at another agency, just because it's been tripped up in what might otherwise have proved to be a very successful campaign. After all, the same thing could have happened – might one day soon happen – to us. Maybe I'm being a bit generous here, but that's the way I feel.

Hakuhodo is said to have offered to return the $5 million it spent on campaign production costs to its client. Kirin will probably accept the offer, but whether Hakuhodo wants to wring this money out of Katsu Productions remains to be seen. The film company's said to be deeply in debt already.

Katsu's wife has been appearing in a skin-cleaner TV campaign that we're handling here in Asatsu. Our client has asked us to lay her off for three months until this business blows over, although it's been good enough to continue to pay her fee (*gara*) during this period. Another point that might interest you is that Kirin's shares have been falling on the Tokyo Stock Exchange. We had a phone call from an American investment banker earlier this morning, asking whether we're in any way connected with the Katsu business. He knew we had an account with Kirin and was trying to work out whether our own stock market position might be adversely affected by what has happened.

These fragments of talk bring to light a number of different issues. Firstly, although advertising likes to make frequent use of celebrities in advertising campaigns of all kinds, there are potential perils in the so-called 'synergy effect' created by the celebrity endorser between a corporation and its product,[25] and the knock-on effect regarding share prices.[26] Secondly, they highlight corporate fear of negative publicity and the fact that, in the world of business, everything must *seem* perfect and proper. Here, as we shall see in the following chapter, impression management is a crucial part of everyday conduct. And thirdly, they promote an otherwise unformulated 'code of honour' among agencies which are otherwise in direct competition with one another for advertising business.

Like many other conversations conducted and listened to in the agency, these *Tales of the Now* include three sources of talk which in Japanese are carefully distinguished: information (*jōhō*), stories pertaining to information (*hanashi*), and gossip (*ura-banashi*, or backstage stories). It is hard to tell as a relatively uninformed and non-involved listener which fragments of the Katsu story are gossip, which factual information, and which stories based on such information, but their mutual influence on one another and overall importance in the advertising world cannot be underestimated. Similarly, it is hard to tell which details are relevant and which not, but what is clear is that employees felt the need to cover all angles of a story, and to consider all their implications in order to be able to frame an appropriate stance and plan, or not plan, appropriate action. It was those who provided an overall vision on the basis of this stream of events and accompanying stories who emerged as the agency's strategists.[27]

The Katsu story is by no means an isolated instance of the business potential created by *Tales of the Now*. Every afternoon, from about five o'clock, the internal telephone lines of the agency were in constant use as people came back from their meetings with clients, media organizations, production houses, and so on and proceeded to let their relevant colleagues know everything that had happened during the working day. At the same time, they relayed pieces of information or gossip that they might have picked up: a potential client's sales manager unhappy with a rival agency's handling of an advertising campaign; a television company worried about the ratings of one of its prime-time programmes and on the lookout for a replacement programme that would satisfy the sponsoring corporation; a client pharmaceutical company said to be developing a new sports drink; a government commission likely to lay down more regulations limiting television advertising by tobacco companies; the marriage of a client advertising manager's son to a rival ad agency CEO's daughter; and so on.

Such information was important because it might affect overall agency activities and strategic planning where (potential) clients were involved. It showed how talk 'explores ways in which organizational stakeholders create a discourse of direction ... to understand and influence one another's actions'.[28] Thus, senior management could use such evolving stories to target the unhappy sales manager, if it felt it appropriate, in the hope that the agency would be asked to participate in a competitive presentation and take over the account in question. The television department could bring off the back burner a programme idea that didn't quite make the cut when the television network concerned was trying to decide at the beginning of the season which new programme proposals to take up, and which not. A smart account manager could get to work on a sports drink brand name and sales concept that he could then propose to his client in a speculative presentation. A marketing executive would be obliged to think of creative ways to re-channel his tobacco company client's advertising money effectively. An account group would be better served soliciting accounts from clients other than the one whose advertising manager's son had just married a rival agency's CEO's daughter; and so forth. If successful, such plans that stemmed from *Tales of the Now* were later transformed into *Tales of the Past* that stressed opportunities perceived and taken, creative thinking, smart initiatives, the value of interpersonal networking, and so forth.

Thirdly, *Tales of the Now* brought to the surface a number of organizational tensions *within* the agency, as well as *between* the agency and other players in the world of advertising. One example concerns gender relations and the difficulties faced by women employees in a Japanese corporation like Asatsu. Take the following extended conversation involving four young women told by a senior male manager to take me out to a 'harem lunch':

A: We're supposed to be equal with men, you know, in terms of working conditions and pay. But you'd never believe it, the way they carry on and order us about.

B: That's true. When I first joined the agency and went through the training programme for new recruits, we were all equal. We felt a sense of camaraderie with the young men who'd come into Asatsu with us.

A: Then, yes. But not later. Once we were assigned our divisions and started work properly, the men always seemed to get given the interesting jobs, didn't they, while all we were told to do was photocopy, post letters, get more stationery and do all the other everyday chores the men never did for themselves.

C: Of course, some women in the agency are happy to play along with the caring role assigned them, but most of us these days would prefer to do something different and show what we're worth.

A: But if we kick up a fuss, we know what'll happen.

C: Yeah. Find ourselves shunted even further aside and made to do even more boring jobs.

B: That's why the best thing to do is to keep quiet and hope that a few fun jobs will come our way.

C: Like the occasional trip abroad on agency business.

A: Or entertaining a visiting professor to a harem lunch! Harem lunch! I ask you. What's going on in that man's mind?

D: Still, the salaries are quite good, aren't they?

A: True, but that's only to make up for the status that we lose by working in the advertising industry in the first place. You know how things are. If we were living in the feudal period, we'd be placed at the very bottom of the four-class system. Like the outcastes. Samurai, peasant, artisan, merchant and … advertising agency!

This conversation, recorded in a basement restaurant in Shinbashi during a weekday lunch hour, brings to the fore a number of problems highlighted by scholars writing about the Japanese employment system: the discrepancy between ideals and reality in company employment practices; the continued sexism in male employees' everyday behaviour; and the attitude of determination 'to grin and bear it' that Japanese women generally have adopted, or felt obliged to adopt.[29]

Another topic that elicited dissatisfaction was financial reward and the fact that the agency was a listed company on the Tokyo Stock Exchange:

All the agency's top management holds shares in Asatsu. And this affects the way they make decisions, in the sense that it pushes top management towards a kind of 'safety' policy, rather than embarking upon an adventurous strategy that might make a loss. That's because their real concern is with ensuring that share prices aren't affected by anything they do. The bottom line is that it's not the agency's future that concerns them so much as their own private wealth.

This six-monthly bonus only comes to 5.2 months this December. Last year, we got 6.4 months. You may think that's quite a lot, but we don't get paid overtime at Asatsu, so those who work here deserve more than most. The trouble is, this year the finance people made a big loss in their dealings on the stock market. I've got a friend who's in the trade, and his company compiled a secret list of companies that had made heavy losses with the stock market crash. Asatsu came out near the top.

Whether such grumblings were justified or not is hard to tell, but they reinforce the general point that there was rarely any *single* story in the agency, but a potentially unlimited number of them circulating around an event.[30] *Tales of the Now* could be quickly extended, expanded, countered or contradicted. They tended to be told with particular purposes or interests in mind, varying according to audience and context as individual actors (re)positioned themselves vis-à-vis one another. Such talk, therefore, always had its alternative versions organized around different plots.[31]

Tales of Reproduction

What I call *Tales of Reproduction* were a kind of 'present perfect' mode of talk that brought together stories of both present and past in such a way that those working in Asatsu could 'reproduce' and thus actively structure their working environment,[32] the organization to which they belonged, and the other organizations with which they came into daily contact.

As implied by their designation, *Tales of Reproduction* recycled particular issues and kept them at the forefront of employees' collective consciousness. As such, they contributed to a 'discourse' that helped people working with all kinds of different colleagues on numerous disparate activities to create and sustain Asatsu as an 'imagined community.'[33]

The focal point of this kind of talk was the advertising account and it was the continuous circulation of accounts among agencies that fuelled talk among those employed in the world of advertising as they took stock of positions and position-takings. One of the best examples of this kind of tale emerged out of the ongoing discussions surrounding the agency's apparent *failure* to hold onto a prestigious account involving a prestigious European automobile manufacturer (which I shall call by a pseudonym, PKW) and mentioned earlier on in this chapter.[34]

Soon after I started my research, I heard about PKW and how Asatsu, against all odds, had won this blue-chip account. It was one of the agency's success stories that the new recruits heard about during their training induction at the beginning of April. By early summer, however, several people in the Marketing and Account Services Divisions were shaking their heads glumly. It seemed that all was not well and that the client had invited Asatsu to take part in a competitive presentation in October, along with two of its main rivals: Dentsu and Hakuhodo. Asatsu hadn't the slightest hope of winning the presentation, it was said, and the International Division was about to lose its prime account.

The stories that were told during the next weeks were various. One emergent theme, recounted under *Tales of the Past*, highlighted how, against all odds, the agency had originally won the account. Another dominant theme concerned what had gone wrong and why Asatsu had been ordered to participate in a competitive presentation together with its main rivals. Here two story strands emerged, both focusing more on the ongoing present, than on the past. One highlighted the 'foreignness' of the European client, the 'special' nature of the Japanese market and Japan's advertising industry, and foreigners' presumed failure to come to terms with or accept 'cultural difference'. This tale was reproduced as a means towards sustaining the idea that the Japanese market was 'different' from other markets and therefore required the expertise of specifically 'Japanese' advertising agencies like Asatsu.

> PKW's a hard taskmaster. It doesn't really understand or appreciate all the time and trouble that the account team's been taking on its behalf.

> It's a pretty arrogant company and really 'bad mannered' (*gyōgi ga warui*). It's pushed the account team – especially those on the creative side – into working so hard that most of the people there are suffering from stress in one form or another. And that doesn't help either agency or client.

> PKW spends its whole time complaining about the fact that Asatsu's handling a large proportion of the Toyobishi Motor Corporation's business. It won't accept the fact that that's the way things are done in Japan. And anyway, Toyobishi's recently signed a tie-up agreement with PKW to share certain sales outlets and to develop engine technology together. So what's the big deal? Asatsu keeps its two clients' businesses in different buildings and there's no interaction between the separate account teams that I ever heard of.

The other homed in on the account manager and his perceived failure to target the right person (that is, the person with real power) in the European automobile manufacturer's Japanese office. This part of the tale of reproduction thus highlighted what an 'ad man' ought to be. It also brought out agency staff's subconscious preference for 'Japanese' employment practices ('permanent' employment rather than job hopping), and, by implication, notions of trust and corporate loyalty that such practices were seen to encourage.

> The trouble is the PKW account manager isn't an ad man at all. He's really no more than an automobile businessman. He was brought in from Toyobishi when Asatsu first won the PKW account because people here felt we needed someone who really knew the car market in Japan.

> 'Mr Automobile', as some of us call him, made a crucial mistake. He targeted the wrong man in the client company. An account manager's job is to find out who the decision maker is and then cultivate him assiduously. That's what human chemistry's all about. And then, if something for some reason does go wrong, the target man can put in a good word for the agency and bail it out of difficulty.
> In the case of PKW, Mr Automobile targeted one of the subsidiary company's vice-presidents. And it was this Japanese guy who he proceeded to develop relations with.

But – whether consciously or not, I'm not in a position to say – Mr Automobile ignored the European sales manager working under the vice-president. This was a costly error of judgement. After all, it was the European who was in charge of day-to-day business matters. And it was the European who had a direct line back to his HQ in Frankfurt, or wherever. Mr Automobile mistook authority for power. The vice- president may have been senior in rank, but he didn't make the important decisions.

I guess the European sales manager felt personally slighted at being ignored by Asatsu's account manager. And then he transformed it into a general dissatisfaction with Asatsu's work on behalf of PKW, and persuaded his bosses back in Europe to call for a competitive presentation.

If we're going to have any chance at all of retaining this account, we've got to take Mr Automobile off it. I mean, completely off it. But the bosses have vetoed the idea. It doesn't bode too well for our chances in the presentation.

This recycling talk was produced and reproduced throughout the hectic five weeks during which Asatsu prepared for the presentation, in the full knowledge that it did not stand a chance of winning its client's approval. Not only did the story emphasize the perceived importance of the 'ad man', it provided crucial ideological back-up to senior management's decision to spare no effort or expense in its preparations for the competitive presentation, so that the client might eventually come to realize just how hard-working, how business-like and how ethically steadfast Asatsu was. In this way, the account itself became a source of pride for all those working in the agency – especially when PKW, clearly impressed by Asatsu's presentation, found itself unable to award the account to either of the agency's rivals without ordering the other two agencies to compete again. Thus, what it may have lost in financial terms, Asatsu recouped in corporate pride and public relations, because word of what was going on became the talking point of other agencies and media organizations alike. This is what recycling talk and stories are all about: they are ethical reflections on the world of advertising as a whole.

A Storytelling Organization

In his analysis of organizational storytelling, Gabriel suggests that 'organizations do not appear to be a natural habitat of storytelling.'[35] Certainly, almost all of the examples cited by David Boje fail to arouse interest in terms of plot, characters, narration, poetic elaboration, and so on.[36] At the same time, however, Gabriel's definition of what constitutes a story is much more comprehensive, and therefore exclusive, than that offered by most, if not all, other scholars.[37] Two or three of the tales outlined in this chapter meet all of his criteria; most others do not. Nevertheless, I think it reasonable to suggest that, as an advertising agency, Asatsu – like a number of other creative industry organizations producing animation, fashion, film, popular music and entertainment generally – is an organization founded on storytelling.[38]

In terms of the actual works that it carries out, an advertising agency is a storytelling organization in three interrelated ways. Firstly, as we have seen in many of the examples cited in this chapter, there is talk about accounts themselves and the intricate and difficult relations that accounts create between agency and client, as well as between client and media, and agency and media. Such talk is for the most part characteristic of what is known about organizations and storytelling elsewhere. *Tales of the Past*, *Tales of the Now*, and *Tales of Reproduction* in this respect confirm Schwartzman's summary of stories as important for:

> (a) communicating historical experiences and providing individuals with a way to weave this experience into discussions of current activities; (b) distinguishing one's organization as the best and/or worst and also for stereotyping other organizations; (c) socializing new members into an organization; (d) documenting successes and failures and drawing conclusions (morals) from these examples; (e) indirectly communicating information to individuals about a range of issues that may be too sensitive or threatening to discuss directly; and, finally, (f) stories may be most important because they shape and sustain individuals' images of the organization in which they work.[39]

In the case of the advertising agency Asatsu, stories also helped employees to:

1. Develop a sense of what it meant as an individual to be a member of a profession and a *professional*.
2. Think strategically and participate in their organization's *strategic development*.
3. Situate their organization within the broader *business context* of the *industry* in which it functioned, as well as within.
4. A broader *cultural context* that included other *national* corporate organizations.

Secondly, the kind of marketing analysis carried out by the agency in its preparations for every advertising campaign also tells a story about and builds up a picture of different kinds of targeted consumers. This we saw in the Frontier account where consumers were categorized in terms of two distinct audiences. One, the 'outer audience group', consisted of people aged between twenty and thirty years (older than Sony's customers) who were categorized as 'steady' rather than 'trend-conscious' in their tastes. This group was in an upper-middle socio-economic bracket, already owned entertainment-oriented VTR players, and was in some way influential in the development of information technology. But it was also unable generally to distinguish what qualities made Frontier products different from those of its competitors, and was likely to categorize Frontier as a 'mini Sony'. The 'inner audience group', on the other hand, was demarcated solely on the grounds that its members worked in different parts of Frontier's organization, both in Japan and elsewhere abroad. All the creative ideas – the so-called perspiration, nature, and other series prepared – were designed to appeal to these two audiences.

Rather more detailed information and stories about consumers were made by Asatsu staff in their recommendations to a skiwear company, which I will call by the pseudonym of Pistela. In a consumer survey, the agency began to put together a consumer profile which suggested that Pistela users were generally neither beginners nor experts, but mid-level when it came to skiing (which may well be why they were influenced by product endorsements featuring world cup skiers). They got their information about products from specialist ski magazine articles, rather than advertising per se, but were also quite strongly influenced by the recommendations of friends when it came to buying ski equipment. Brand name was important, of course, but purchasing decisions were ultimately based on how well a product fitted.

The agency's account team suggested that one strategy should be to establish brand identity to enable future corporate identity and the communication concept proposed with this in mind was 'beauty as sexiness'. One of the proposed advertising approaches focused on 'young sexy women' and 'sexy people' and was described in the following way:

> Young women living naturally and enjoying their freedom exude a healthy sexiness in all the ways they talk and comport themselves. They also possess a vitality that make[s] them appear masters of their own universe.

> When people get together to have fun and party with friends while skiing, one can always find Pistela. The aficionados of Pistela products can be identified as 'Pistelans' in describing a refreshingly healthy and sexy scene of ski enjoyment.

Thirdly, as hinted at in the last example, the creative strategy and images based on market analysis tell stories about the corporations and/or products being advertised. As David Ogilvy has remarked, 'There are no dull products, only dull writers.'[40] The product or corporation, therefore, has to be turned into a 'hero'. Take the 'sexy performance' approach that was also recommended:

> Jumping and turning through snow as one with the winds and light to a gracefully powerful finish, Pistela ski boots deliver precise response to the skier's will. Possessing superb quality and reliability resulting from the pursuit of performance, Pistela boots represent the full confidence of skiers. The sexy, functional beauty of Pistela ski boots and their aggressive dynamism will be portrayed in a hard-edged, yet beautiful manner through skiing scenes.

In general, of course, the aim of much advertising is to link product (and/or advertiser) to (the idealized) consumer. This was the case with the agency's 'sexy skills' and 'sexy athlete' approaches:

Sweat glistening on the forehead, brows furrowed in deep concentration, the body pushed to the ultimate … One can easily appreciate the sexiness of an intensely athletic scene.

World Cup ski competitors stage battles decided on mere one-hundredths of a second under rigorous conditions. In every fraction of their competition time, they maximally represent a breathtakingly beautiful sexiness. In this realm of the chosen ones at the apex of the skiing world, Pistela's ski boots can be appealed [*sic*] as vital equipment precisely responding to the will of the competitors and fulfilling their trust and passion.

There are two main characters, the athlete taking on the World Cup challenge, and a woman praying for his glory. The athlete exhibits his masterly skiing skills, and the woman aggressively drives a car. As the race progresses, one can hear the quickening pulse of the couple, and see the deft movements of the athlete's skis and the woman's spinning tyres. By striking out the close, almost conspiratorial relationship between the athlete and the woman, the Pistela boots can be shown to be as good a partner to the athlete as the woman is.

These kinds of stories are accompanied by visual images which themselves – like the eye patch sported by the model for Hathaway shirts – have 'story appeal' and attract attention.[41] They can be found buried in every advertising campaign, even though it is often hard for us to recognize that the images we see are formulated on the basis of stories that emerge from marketing research. It is recommendations like the ones detailed above that bring a whole new nuance to the meaning of 'storyboards' used by advertising agencies when they present their creative work to their clients.[42]

Conclusion

In theoretical terms, this chapter is framed as a tale of the organizing processes out of which actors' sense of organization emerges and is acted out.[43] It shows how Asatsu, like many other organizations all over the world, is 'a collective storytelling system in which the performance of stories is a key part of members' sense making and a means to allow them to supplement individual memories with institutional memory'.[44] Talk is the agency's lifeblood. It enables those working there to discover and affirm 'their shared goals, many agendas, environmental uncertainties, potential coalitions, and areas of actual conflict'. Talk constitutes 'the very *structuring* of the organization'.[45]

The kind of structuring that went on in Asatsu during my fieldwork covered a number of different fronts. On the one hand, it concerned the identity of employees and a notion of the agency's corporate culture – in the sense of what distinguished it from other agencies and players in the advertising industry. This structuring focused ultimately on positioning. On the other hand, it laid bare certain potential points of conflict – gender relations within the agency, or tensions between Japanese and Western ways of conducting business – and tried to work them back into the everyday lives of employees in such a way that the latter could come to terms with the ongoing anomalies they encountered. In general, the structuring process here was more concerned with the field of Japanese advertising as a whole and the in-built tensions that emerged from the split- account system and agency-client and agency-media relations.

In general, however, there was little glossing over of different accounts of stories told in the agency, if only because people needed to be able to get every conceivable angle on what went on in order to be able to think laterally and come up with different and exciting advertising and marketing ideas. Senior management, therefore, did not practise the kind of totalizing storytelling that David Boje found in Disney,[46] although there was a concerted effort on their part to help employees cope with tensions like stress and intercultural communication that resulted from working in the advertising world.

At the same time my involvement in Asatsu's presentation preparations for the Frontier account emphasized the fact that there is a world of difference between managerial and public relations exercises, on the one hand, and the near chaotic, ad hoc processes that characterize the daily lives of people working in the advertising business, on the other. Although, in this case there seemed to be an overall coherence to the stories emerging among members of the account team, my later participation in an unsuccessful presentation to PKW revealed certain chinks in the agency's art of self-presentation.

For example, among the stories circulating about Asatsu's difficulties with PKW, one version claimed that the client was looking for a way to get out of its business arrangement with the agency because the latter handled the account of Toyobishi, a rival Japanese car manufacturer. Thus, it didn't matter whether the PKW account manager, 'Mr Automobile', had or had not failed to target the right person in the client company. The result would still have been the same: an end to Asatsu's involvement in the PKW account.

In this context, we might note David Boje's comment that:

> The storytelling organization consists of many struggling stories, each a particular framing of reality being chased by wandering and fragmented audiences. In its plurivocality, each story masks a diversity and a multiplicity of voices. As organizations evolve, new voices tell the organizational story lines, often changing the meaning of the stories or invoking change within the organization by revising the old stories.[47]

The forms taken by such stories and talk and the functions they had (foreign versus Japanese; advertising versus other professions; male versus female employees) were as varied as the particular interests and purposes they were designed to serve. In this respect, we might say that an unlimited number of *relations* exist between the different forms of talk – *Tales of the Past*, *Tales of the Now*, and *Tales of Reproduction* – that I have outlined here and that it is in these relations – or 'nets of collective action'– that the very notion of an 'organization' emerges.[48]

At the same time, stories also clearly constituted 'micropractices of power'.[49] Not only was there management by particular individuals in the telling of stories.[50] Those with access to information (primarily through personally cultivated networks) were respected (for what was known as their 'broad face') and, depending on their ability to transform informational content into strategic practice, gained authority as a result. Thus, even those in subordinate positions – like the women who kindly accompanied me to a 'harem lunch' – jostled for control of what was being said (as can be seen in A's contributions to the conversation recorded). This is the subject matter of the ethnography of speaking.[51]

Finally, in a discussion of corporate culture and what they call the 'uniqueness paradox', Jo-Ann Martin and her colleagues have isolated seven story types that they see as characterizing the content of tales told in corporations.[52] We have come across some of these – like 'Is the big boss human?' and 'How will the organization deal with obstacles?' – during the course of this chapter. Others, however – like 'Will I get fired?' and 'Will the organization help me when I move?' – are missing, presumably because they do not fit in with ideals of the Japanese employment system that have favoured 'permanent' employment and regularly taken care of employees transferred to other parts of the country or world. Moreover, while Martin and her fellow authors give examples of both positive and negative versions of each story type, in Asatsu generally stories were positive, rather than negative. This may well have been because the company was doing very well at the time of my research. It was reinforced by a positive, Mencian attitude towards people and situations on the part of the CEO and all employees in Asatsu.

Such cultural differences were backed up by a certain difference in story emphases from those noted by Martin and her co-authors. For example, while the issue of in/security was notably lacking in stories about the agency's internal organization (it was certainly there, though, in tales of what was going on *out*side Asatsu), other considerations like long-/short-term outlook, ethics, and the tension between individual and collectivity (from corporation down to team) were very much present in employees' stories.

At the same time, one major difference in content noted in this chapter has been the way in which agency stories focussed on the strategic implications of events in the field of advertising in general. Strategy was in many cases the be-all and end-all of storytelling. It was also, as we shall now see, a crucial element in Asatsu's interactive practices.

−4−

Impression Management

One of the obvious things about talk is that all of us most of the time use language for the purpose of what Irving Goffman has called 'impression management.'[1] This kind of performative activity may occur during classroom interaction, as part of a conversation with a member of the opposite sex at a party, in bartering exchanges in a bazaar-style marketplace, or during the course of an advertising agency's presentation to a client. In different social contexts, different criteria are brought to bear on what is thought to be the most appropriate, and thus effective, way of impressing others: 'deep' and 'intelligent' questions in class, humorous banter at a party, sharp bargaining in a shopping purchase, and an overall sense of 'professionalism' in a presentation.

Picking up on Goffman's discussion of how people present themselves in their everyday lives, the anthropologist Victor Turner argues that 'man is a self-performing animal – his performances are, in a way, *reflexive*, in performing he reveals himself to himself.'[2] Consequently, performance is 'the basic stuff of social life'. Distinguishing between 'social' and 'cultural' performances, Turner starts by isolating cultural performances as units of observation, since they are central to and continually recur in people's social lives. Cultural performances make use of certain modes of readily understandable verbal and non-verbal communication (what he calls 'cultural media'), which are orchestrated and often directed by a kind of 'master of ceremonies', who may be a conductor of an orchestra, a director of a theatre play, or a priest at a religious ceremony.[3]

Now, in certain important respects, an advertising agency's presentation to a client may be seen as a cultural performance. It is performed regularly as and when a corporation decides to hire a (new) agency to prepare its advertising campaigns for it, and it is recurrent – for agencies, in particular, but often for their dissatisfied clients, too. It is orchestrated by the person who, having been assigned to make the 'pitch', must ensure that all media used – from marketing statistics and media analysis to creative ideas with their print and TV storyboards – come together in an appropriate and persuasive manner. By blending statistical data with visual ideas, the presenter, ideally, creates a one-off performance that cannot be repeated exactly in ensuing cultural performances for, again ideally, while it reflects the client's orientation and vision of itself and its products, the creative ideas can sketch out what copywriters and art directors believe to be more apt and novel 'designs for living'.[4] In this way, a presentation allows the cultural flow of commodity culture to fold back on itself as an agency expresses 'in subjunctive mood' a series of suppositions, hypotheses, desires and possibilities (rather than actual facts) enabling a client to see a new way forward from its present 'indicative state'.[5]

When an advertising agency makes a presentation, it implicitly requests its would-be client to take seriously the impression that is fostered before it as part of its cultural performance. The client is asked to believe that the character of the agency actually possesses the attributes it appears to possess, that the task it is performing in terms of market analysis and strategic communication ideas will have the consequences implicitly claimed for it and that, in general, things are what they seem.[6]

In this chapter, I intend to follow the consequences of Goffman's and Turner's ideas about social and cultural performances (and performances about performances about performances), in the light of two competitive presentations in which Asatsu found itself: one, its successful pitch for the international account of Frontier; the other its failure to retain the prestigious PKW automobile account, mentioned in the previous chapter.

Dramaturgical Performances

In his final discussion of the analytical context of his study of *The Presentation of Self in Everyday Life*, Goffman suggests that an organization (or, in his words, 'establishment') can be viewed in a number of different ways: (1) *technically*, in terms of its in/efficiency in achieving defined objectives as an intentionally organized system; (2) *politically*, in terms of demands made by participants on one another, together with social controls and sanctions imposed; (3) *structurally*, in terms of horizontal and vertical status divisions and the social relations emerging from such divisions; (4) *culturally*, in terms of moral values held by members and influencing their activity; and – his own addition – (5) *dramaturgically*, in terms of techniques of impression management employed, problems arising from their use, and the identity and inter-relationships of performance teams operating in the organization concerned.[7] It is the dramaturgical aspect of an agency's presentation that I wish to pursue here.

Let us start by recapping what a presentation is in the world of advertising. Any corporation wishing to use an agency to create an advertising campaign on its behalf expects that agency, at one stage or another, to present its ideas for that campaign. This kind of presentation can be more or less formal, depending on the organization concerned, its relations with the selected agency, the personnel involved in the final decision-making process, and so on. But the most formal kind of presentation is that in which several agencies compete for the attention of the would-be advertiser and try to persuade the latter that *their* market analysis and creative ideas are in some way better than those of their competitors. It is for this reason called a competitive presentation.

An advertising agency's participation in a competitive presentation may be described as a dramaturgical performance. There is a lot to support this view. Like many other service occupations which also put on for their customers a performance illuminated with dramatic expressions of one sort or another,[8] an advertising agency has to convince a client of its strategic ability, creative expression, professional competence and overall business integrity – all, like a play, film or concert – in the space of approximately two hours. And, as with a real play enacted on stage, the director has to ensure that the marketing plot and creative storyline are strong enough to carry the production through to the end of the presentation, while the actors (as we saw in Chapter 1) have to rehearse their parts so that the actual performance runs smoothly and is met with rapturous applause at the final curtain.

There are several other features supporting the idea of a presentation as a dramaturgical cultural performance. For one, there is the frame in which it takes place. Performances in general tend to be given in a 'highly bounded region, to which boundaries with respect to time are often added'.[9] A presentation does not take place in public and is therefore a form of 'secluded liminality',[10] which allows a select group of people in both agency and client company to isolate themselves from their colleagues, as they go through a performance that will reclassify them or not as 'contracted agency' and 'client' respectively.

Dramatic performances of all kinds – fashion shows, art auctions, book fairs, pop concerts, and so on, as well as the kinds of rituals studied by anthropologists – are 'both a ritual and unique event', with 'fixed trysting places' set apart in terms of time, place, setting and props.[11] 'The decorations and permanent fixtures in a place where a particular performance is usually given, as well as the performers and performance usually found there, tend to fix a kind of spell over it; even when the customary performance is not being given in it, the place tends to retain some of its front region character.'[12] Asatsu's presentation room, for example, had but a single window that opened up onto a closed roof area that was decorated as a Japanese garden. There were no clocks on the walls; no telephones to the outside world. Its chairs were plush, and its single long table was expansive and well polished, affording those present a sense of their own significance.[13] Although it could be put to other purposes, such as for the meeting when Tanaka came to formally award Asatsu the Frontier account, the presentation room gave off a certain 'hallowed exclusion' in its atmosphere – in large part because, like a church, it was *not* used that much, and then generally only for special purposes.

Then there is the 'pitch'. As in most theatrical performances of this nature, the lead actor – the account executive or creative director who makes the presentation

– is at centre stage. He expresses what he wishes to convey during the interaction, by infusing his pitch with 'signs that dramatically highlight and portray confirmatory facts that might otherwise remain unapparent or obscure'.[14] It is his 'pitch' which, like the auctioneer's chant, acts as the 'theme song of the performance'.[15] He will thus modulate his voice to conform to the contents of what is being said – moving quickly through those sections of the pitch which are based on the client's own orientation to the agency, going more slowly when the account team's own analysis is highlighted, and pausing dramatically before showing a new slide that illustrates a 'Big Idea' of some sort or another. In this way, he orchestrates the rhythm of the presentation, establishing its cadence, moulding the potentially disjointed spheres of media, marketing and creative ideas into an ongoing harmonious process. He also manages the participants, giving them their cues where necessary, by steering them in the direction of what he wants them to see, and by being ever ready to provide the slightest break in his pitch to enable an eager executive to ask the question that he wants asked.[16] As the department chief handling the PKW account remarked, 'There has to be interaction between agency and client. Otherwise, the presentation will be sterile.'

There are two conflicting issues here. On the one hand, an advertising agency's account team is showing a client a finished product, and the presenter knows that he and his colleagues will be judged on the basis of the well-polished and packaged creative ideas that are put forward.[17] He knows, therefore, when to drop a point in response to a client's raised eyebrow, or to pursue one because of a smile.[18] At the same time, there is a need to make invisible work visible and to have noted what may otherwise go only partly observed by the client. Consequently, the presenter is from time to time tempted to reveal the hard work that has been going on behind the scenes during the period leading up to the presentation itself – as when Ueda spun a little story about the account team's hesitation over using the tag lines provided for it by Frontier and its consequent search for something that might be, perhaps, more 'cutting-edge'. Both *The Pulse of Entertainment* and *The Art of Entertainment* seemed somehow to constrain the collective imagination of the creative team. It was only when, after much brainstorming and soul-searching, *It's in the Name* popped up as a viable alternative that the creative ideas placed before everyone today slotted into place.

This principle of making the invisible visible applies to the person making the presentation.[19] The pitch itself has to be smooth, communicative and flawless. But this is not enough. The account executive concerned should make it apparent that he is performing well, so that the client will be consciously impressed. He needs also to give the impression that his pitch, and the contact he has with the client during the presentation, have something very special and unique about them. Thus, he may inject on occasion a 'personal touch'– a joke or frame-breaking comment on some previous contact between him and a member of the client company that will be appreciated by all present. This need explains Ueda's perspiration and virtual collapse at the end of the Frontier presentation. That he was successful in making the invisible visible can be seen in the fact that it later elicited humorous but admiring comment from Tanaka when he came to inform Asatsu officially that the agency had been awarded the Frontier account.

But presentations are not *just* plays, put on by actors for an audience that pays for the entertainment and then goes home to lead its multiple lives. Participants on both agency and client sides in a presentation are trying to establish a permanent business relationship that will continue after the performance is over. A presentation therefore offers more than the merely dramaturgical and so may also be classed as what the anthropologist, Arjun Appadurai, has termed a 'tournament of value'. These he defines as:

> Complex periodic events that are removed in some culturally well-defined way from the routine of economic life. Participation in them is ... both a privilege of those in power and an instrument of status contests between them. The currency of such tournaments is also ... set apart through well understood cultural diacritics ... What is at issue ... is not just status, rank, fame, or reputation of actors, but the disposition of the central tokens of value in the society in question. Finally, though such tournaments of value occur in special times and places, their forms and outcomes are always consequential for the more mundane realities of power and value in ordinary life.[20]

Tournaments of value are by no means limited to advertising presentations, but may be found in a number of different arenas in contemporary industrialized societies – particularly, I think, among creative industries producing fashion, art, music, film, and so on. One example is the various haute couture and prêt-à-porter fashion shows held every six months in Paris, London, Milan, New York and Tokyo. Another is the kind of auction put on with accompanying publicity by Sotherby's, Christie's and other art auctioneers. A third is the annual media events celebrating the achievements of different branches of the entertainment industry: the Grammy awards for music; 'Oscars' for the Hollywood film industry; the Cleos in advertising; and so on. To these we may add such extravaganzas as the Miss World and Miss Universe beauty competitions; the Eurovision Song Contest; various major museum art exhibitions; film festivals themselves (in Cannes, Venice, and so on); and the Nobel prize-giving ceremonies. All of these are cultural performances. All of them are dramaturgical in form. All of them exhibit somewhat more than meets the eye.

Like art auctions and fashion shows, Oscars and Grammy Awards, advertising agency presentations are part and parcel of the processes that serve to define and maintain the advertising community as a whole. They involve questions of membership of that community, manage the interpersonal relationships of participants and regulate behaviour during performances (including in-group language and dress codes) (Smith 1989: 51). There are, of course, greater and lesser competitive presentations, but they occur only periodically, and they are always marked by the fact that agencies are *invited* to participate in them. The latter devote a lot of time and energy, therefore, to persuading (would-be) clients that they are worthy of inclusion in advertising's 'community of the privileged' by being allowed to make a presentation.[21] Their modes of persuasion (invitations to expensive dinners, exclusive bars or rounds of golf, together with the handing out of free tickets to *sumō* tournaments or the latest opera) are similar to the 'solicitary gifts' offered and accepted among (would-be) participants in the *kula* ring,[22] as well as to the lavish parties thrown for clients by haute couture houses to launch their latest perfumes (as captured on BBC television in *The Look*). In other words, human behaviour does not seem to change much, even with the benefits of 'civilization' or globalization.

The 'currency' of the presentation is the account. It is the fact that it is an account awarded by a particular corporation that counts, and not money, as such. As the well-known designer, Karl Lagerfeld, has put it when talking about fashion shows: 'I don't buy. You don't buy. I propose.'[23] Moreover, the account is not subject to laws of supply and demand, but to personal taste. As we shall see again in the following chapter on creativity, an account team in an advertising agency will therefore include a particular tag line, celebrity name or creative idea, even though those concerned realize that it may not be entirely appropriate, because they have found out that it appeals to a decision-making executive in the client company. In many ways, therefore, 'exchange value' is not offered or proposed so much as 'wagered'.[24]

Moreover, as in the art auction and the *kula* ring, the object being exchanged provides each new owner not simply with economic profit, but with legitimacy in his or her respective community. An Oscar for Best Supporting Actor, a Grammy for Best Female Vocalist, a Cleo for Copywriter of the Year – each of these, like the awarding of an account following a presentation, results in a kind of *rite de passage* as a new social identity is forged (although this newly acquired 'cultural capital' can be quickly exchanged for an increase in financial remuneration for services rendered). The account in question becomes endowed with a history, written up in industry publications, and known to all concerned in the world of advertising. Like a French oil painting or a Western Pacific island (*kula*) arm shell,[25] an account thus takes on a certain pedigree – a provenance which includes such details as the account's value; by which agency it has been won; from whom, when, and why it was transferred; for how long it was then maintained, and with what effect. When that provenance raises the account to the state of being desired by *every* agency on the block, it becomes blue chip – equivalent in the world of advertising to a Leonardo da Vinci, Rembrandt, Picasso or Cézanne.

It is precisely because of the provenance with which each object is endowed that its circulation is not fortuitous. Consider, for example, the chain of events that was set into motion when Asatsu lost the PKW account to Dentsu. Almost immediately, PKW's biggest European competitor and rival, whose account had hitherto been handled by Dentsu, made public its dissatisfaction at its agency taking on the PKW account, and called for its own competitive presentation. Although Asatsu managed to get itself invited to participate, this account (the second largest among foreign automobile companies) was in the end awarded to Japan's second largest agency, Hakuhodo. As a result the *third* largest foreign car manufacturer, hitherto handled by Hakuhodo, decided to call for *its* competitive presentation. Again, Asatsu was invited to participate and this time it was awarded the account. As a result, within two to three years it succeeded in procuring the account of another major European car manufacturer, and thereby maintained its legitimacy as a top-ranking Japanese advertising agency able to serve foreign clients. Given that Asatsu itself had risen up the agency rankings during this period, the final distribution of European car manufacturer advertising accounts paralleled in financial value and prestige the ranking of the advertising agencies awarded those accounts.

This example reveals very clearly that there is more than an aimless shifting of accounts among agencies in the advertising industry. Like art auctions and the *kula*, presentations are designed to reproduce 'markets, player positions, and collective wisdom'. They do not generate new values, classifications, social relationships or reputations so much as modify and sustain those that already exist.[26]

Social Drama

Another way of looking at the presentation as a dramaturgical performance is to see it as part of a *social drama*. A social drama is 'an objectively isolable sequence of social interactions of a conflictive, competitive or agonistic type',[27] and it is during the course of every drama that stories, like the ones we looked at in the previous chapter, emerge and flourish.

Victor Turner argues that the form of the social drama is universal, although it is culturally elaborated in different ways in different societies.[28] This universal structure consists of 'a regular course of events which can be grouped in successive phases of public action'.[29] These phases consist, firstly, of a *breach* of regular, norm-governed relations – a 'symbolic transgression'[30] – that takes place when, for example, an account manager goes over the head of a European sales manager who feels slighted and reports his dissatisfaction back to head office which, in turn, orders its Japan branch office to review its advertising account because sales are not satisfactory.[31] Secondly, a *crisis* occurs within the advertising agency whose members proceed to try to piece together what the breach is that precipitated the review in the first place, and then why it has occurred and who is responsible. People take sides as fault lines are unearthed, and possible sanctions are discussed – as we saw in the previous chapter, where blame for the PKW account mishap was quickly pinned on Mr Automobile and steps were taken to relieve him of responsibility for the account. A sacrificial victim had been found. It is at this point that the dramaturgical nature of the social drama comes into effect, as people begin to use 'dramaturgical language about the language of ordinary role-playing and status-maintenance'[32] which are normally used to communicate everyday business matters.

The third phase consists of *redressive procedures* as those concerned try to heal the breach. These are carried out primarily on two fronts – one within the agency, the other between agency and client. Within the agency, there are one or two informal talks between superordinates and the person or persons responsible for the breach. Mr Automobile, for example, was questioned fairly closely by the head of the International Division who had initially allocated him the position of responsibility for the PKW account and who was therefore himself implicated in Mr Automobile's tactical error in targeting the wrong executive in the client company. He was also questioned by his department chief who had been detailed by the Board of Directors to handle all preparations for the agency's presentation to PKW, and who needed to know as much as possible about the background history of the account and agency-client relations.

At the same time, as an inherent part of the redressive procedures, there was a certain amount of reflection by those not immediately involved in the PKW account upon how they themselves might have acted in similar circumstances, and how they themselves were currently behaving in their current business engagements. This brought into the open certain standards that they should adhere to – in particular, the necessity to ensure that they themselves were targeting the right person in a client company, and that an account executive's attentions should always be spread fairly evenly around other members of a client company who were in touch with the agency for one reason or another. The crisis, in other words, is a clarion call reminding all concerned of the potential problems besetting the conduct of the business in which they are engaged.

Meanwhile, selected persons in the agency in which the social drama is taking place do their utmost to redress the situation by wooing certain members of the client company. Thus, during lunch with the slighted European sales manager, the department chief detailed to make the presentation found himself readily agreeing to a change in account personnel, as well as to his own assumption of overall management of the PKW account, should the client decide to rule in the agency's favour after the competitive presentation. In the meantime, more senior personnel were also making redressive overtures – a domestic account division's senior manager with the client's other (more powerful) vice president; the agency's CEO with the CEO of a Japanese automobile manufacturer, which had been one of Asatsu's most important and prestigious clients over a great many years, but which also, importantly, had recently embarked upon a joint technology-development venture with

PKW. Perhaps a little leverage could be exerted through this link? In this way are lines thrown between the good ship agency and the client dock, from which it has drifted into treacherous waters, in an attempt to secure the two once more.

The presentation itself acts as the final part of these redressive activities, for it is the decision made thereafter which culminates in the fourth and final part of the social drama. Either *reintegration* takes place between agency and client, when the latter decides that, after all, it will continue to retain the former's services. Or, in a more likely scenario, an irreparable *schism* ensues, as a new agency is appointed (as when Asatsu was appointed instead of J&M by Frontier), and existing business relations between the two corporations are severed.[33]

Now, as the last sentence indicates, what is a social drama for one agency and its already existing client is a mere cultural performance for a participating organization that wishes to win the floating account. Thus, in the case of Frontier, Asatsu was merely involved in a dramaturgical performance because the breach had already taken place between Frontier and J&M and was no doubt being followed by a crisis and remedial action on the part of the failed agency – in the same way that, when Asatsu found itself at odds with PKW, it, too, went through successive stages of its own social drama. At the same time, however, Asatsu was able to profit from the social drama taking place between Frontier and J&M, in that the main protagonist for Frontier, Tanaka, undoubtedly relayed information about the drama's unfolding either directly to Ueda or indirectly through colleagues, including the sales manager charged with the execution of domestic advertising, who then passed on information to his opposite number in Asatsu, who could relay it to Ueda and his account team in the International Division. Such information could potentially 'exaggerate, invert, re-form, magnify, minimize, dis-colour, re-colour, even deliberately falsify' social reality in the final cultural performance.[34]

As the above account illustrates, certain common factors are to be found in every social drama. The period of crisis, for example, tends to bring factional struggles, or at least ongoing disagreements within the group, to the surface, while during the redressive stage various mechanisms are employed (ranging from informal advice to formal arbitration or the performance of public ritual) to bring things back on an even keel. Almost invariably, a victim or scapegoat is pinpointed and 'sacrificed' to make up for the group's 'sin' of redressive violence.[35] Whether a social drama ends in reintegration or schism, its closure invariably in some ways alters the structure of the social field in which it takes place.[36] Thus, by winning the Frontier account, Asatsu was able to add one more blue-chip client to its list and raise its overall social capital among competing agencies – in the same way that, by losing the PKW account, it lost some social capital, even though it simultaneously gained some cultural capital because of the way in which it pulled out all the stops in its preparations for the presentation and was seen by others to have gone down fighting gallantly.

So a social drama is clearly a disharmonic social process, arising in a situation of conflict, in which someone or some organization moves to a new place in the social order. In the case of the PKW presentation, for example, an ongoing series of disagreements between the overall head of the agency's International Division, on the one hand, and his immediate subordinate, a department head, on the other, developed into a fairly open power struggle, during which, it was clear, almost all middle-ranking managerial staff sided with the department head. Unlike his immediate superior, this department head had lived and studied in the United States, spoke fluent English, and was generally conversant with Western-style business methods. Although comparatively young for his position, he had always shown excellent tactical skills and was generally respected for his strategic thinking. The divisional head, on the other hand, who had very little understanding of non-Japanese business methods, had appointed Mr Automobile senior manager in charge of the PKW account, apparently against the department head's advice.

Not much had been made of this disagreement until Mr Automobile made his fatal error. But once the crisis occurred, muttered conversations began to take place in various unmanned corners of the agency's buildings, leading fairly promptly to recriminations against the divisional head on the part of middle-ranking managers and rank-and-file employees. The department head, who had the ear of the CEO, but who also wished to play the rebounding ball with a straight bat, felt obliged to point out some of the leadership problems affecting his division to the Board of Directors (on which, as a relatively senior and internationally-oriented manager, he had a seat). As a result, he found himself tacitly placed in charge, although formally his immediate superior continued to head the division. At the same time, however, the latter in almost all certainty saw the writing on the wall, for he quickly developed serious migraine headaches that kept him out of the office, and occasionally in hospital overnight (where doctors could find no remedies or cause), so that the department head 'naturally' found himself formally taking over the reins of power from his superior.

Situations like this are clearly dramatic because 'participants not only do things, they try *to show others what they are doing or have done*',[37] and there is, therefore, quite a lot of playing to the audience at this stage in the social drama – as when the department chief made it clear to all his colleagues that he was not going to usurp the divisional head's position. Moreover, as we have seen both here and in the previous chapter's discussion of advertising talk:

> The meaning of the past is assessed by reference to the present and, of the present by reference to the past; the resultant 'meaningful' decision modifies the group's orientation to or even plans for the future, and these in turn react upon its evaluation of the past. Thus the apprehension of the meaning of life is always relative, and involved in perpetual change.[38]

Social dramas 'occur within groups of persons who share values and interests and who have a real or alleged common history. The main actors are persons for whom the group has a high value priority' (Turner 1981: 145), or for whom it is a 'star group'.

> Only those who feel strongly about their membership in such a group are impelled to enter into relationships with others which become fully 'meaningful,' in the sense that the beliefs, values, norms, and symbols 'carried' in the group's culture become so internalized in a member that they constitute a major part of what s/he might regard as his/her identity.[39]

Given that the agency itself constituted a star group for those concerned, we can then reverse this argument and ask what are the beliefs, values, norms and symbols in an agency that are revealed by the existence of a social drama? One is the emphasis on ensuring continuous and harmonious social interaction between individuals; another the strategic value of targeting a decision maker in a client company; yet another, as was mentioned in the previous chapter, the potential weakness of *zen'in keieishugi* in terms of management structure; but at the same time the importance of not singling out an individual for punishment because of the high value placed on teamwork and co-operation; and so on. In this way, a social drama causes people to reflect upon their star group and the discrepancies that arise between ideal models of business behaviour and its actual practices.

Self Presentation

It will be clear from this analysis of a particular social drama that emerged in Asatsu because of a sudden call for it to compete for the PKW account that all sorts of people in the world of business participate daily in different kinds of impression management, and that ultimately it is *corporations* that try to impress other corporations to enable business deals to go through and profits to be made. It is now time to try to make a link between individuals and organizations at work.

Goffman's discussion of how people present themselves in everyday life starts off by focusing on face-to-face interaction at the level of individuals. I myself have followed this approach by looking at the role of the person making the pitch in a presentation, and by outlining some of the precise calculations he makes in impressing his audience by means of language and other readily understood symbols. But, precisely because he is involved in a dramaturgical performance, the presenter acts on behalf of the advertising agency by which he is employed. Just as Laurence Olivier transformed himself into Richard III on stage, so did Ueda take on the role of Asatsu when making his pitch to members of Frontier.

For this reason, I believe that we may usefully relocate Goffman's argument about theatrical performance at a less micro-sociological level and translate it, where appropriate, into organizational behaviour in general. After all, in business, the way in which an individual expresses him or her self is quickly translated by those present from the level of the individual to that of the organization to which s/he belongs, so that, instead of 'Mr X proposed this', or 'Ms Y did that', those present will say simply 'NHK proposed this', or 'the Asahi Newspaper did that'. Similarly, when referring to corporations which have assigned an advertising account to Asatsu, agency employees will generally say 'the client (*otokuisan*) says this', or cite the name of the company ('Frontier says this'), rather than name the particular individual responsible.[40]

Goffman provides a means by which micro-level social analysis can be shifted to mid-level, and that is by way of his discussion of teams. Most performances, he says, are carried out by a team, that is 'a set of individuals whose intimate cooperation is required if a given projected definition of the situation is to be maintained'.[41] In the case of the presentation, it is the account team which acts as a kind of 'secret society'[42] as it goes about preparing for its final dramaturgical performance. But we should also note that the audience itself constitutes a second team, and that both groupings need to present a team performance during the presentation.[43] It is this meeting of opposing-but-colluding teams that forms the basis of the business *pas de deux* that is to be danced thereafter.

Precisely because business partners tend to be 'adversaries in collusion'[44] the negotiations that take place between two organizations often make use of a shill. A shill is 'someone who acts as though he were an ordinary member of the audience but is in fact in league with the performers'.[45] This was precisely the role adopted by Tanaka as he acted as go-between in pre-presentation dealings between Asatsu and Frontier, and it is the kind of role we find in almost all negotiations between agencies and clients, where one person is designated by his team as the unofficial source of confidential information that will enable a favoured agency to get the nod over its rivals in a competitive presentation. It is the shill 'who appears to be just another unsophisticated member of the audience and who uses his unapparent sophistication in the interests of the performing team'[46] – as when, at the end of the Frontier presentation, Tanaka proceeded to ask a question to which he already knew the answer from previous interaction with the account team, but which he felt that other members of the audience, who did not know, should know.

In an advertising agency's dealings with its client, therefore, the two representatives of performer and audience are to some extent in league with each other. Thus Ueda and his internal account AE colleague, Uchida, were both able to get access to Frontier confidential information and senior management thinking through Tanaka, and to relay them back to their own team as appropriate. But this role in a way made both Ueda and Uchida slightly outside, while being centrally inside, the agency's back-stage team. There were at times discussions among those concerned about what Ueda might relay to Tanaka in regard to agency preparations and ideas (free secrets) and what not (entrusted secrets). Presumably the same went on back stage in Frontier with regard to Tanaka's activities and how much he could and should release to Asatsu, as well as to the competing agency, J&M.

As we have seen above, a presentation is a front which displays consistency and overall coherence and 'which regularly functions in a general and fixed fashion to define the situation for those who observe the performance'.[47] Both teams, therefore, have to observe that front and behave accordingly, even though all kinds of back-stage discussions and deals may have been going on prior to the performance. Although not all members of each team are party to all the different strands of communication taking place between them, they mutually respond to others' expressions and impressions, so that there is a two-way definition of any situation.

> Ordinarily the definitions of the situation projected by the several different participants are sufficiently attuned to one another, so that open contradiction will not occur. I do not mean that there will be the kind of consensus that arises when each individual present candidly expresses what he really feels and honestly agrees with the expressed feelings of the others present. This kind of harmony is an optimistic ideal and in any case is not necessary for the smooth working of society. Rather, each participant is expected to suppress his immediate heartfelt feelings, conveying a view of the situation which he feels the others will be able to find at least temporarily acceptable. The maintenance of this surface of agreement, this veneer of consensus, is facilitated by each participant concealing his own wants behind statements which assert values to which everyone present feels obliged to give lip service ... Together the participants contribute to a single over-all definition of the situation which involves not so much a real agreement as to what exists but rather a real agreement as to whose claims concerning what issues will be temporarily honoured. Real agreement will also exist concerning the desirability of avoiding an open conflict of definitions of the situation.[48]

Although a presentation is a 'collective representation',[49] however, it does not necessarily mean that all members of a team will look the same or behave uniformly. Even in a standard 'salaryman' Japanese company like Frontier, for example, where employees would normally wear dark suits, the most senior person present, Oba, was able to put in his appearance in shirt sleeves (and accompany his entrance with the throwaway line: 'You'd better keep me awake. I've only just come back from New York and am suffering from jet lag'). Similarly, different members of an account team with different functions may well be consistent in manner and appearance with the task that they perform, rather than with one another,[50] thereby conforming to Goffman's observation that 'it is often the case that each member of such a troupe or cast of players may be required to appear in a different light if the team's over-all effect is satisfactory.'[51]

Thus, creative staff often sport eye-catching accessories (silver bracelets, gold rings, tinted glasses) and dress in flamboyant shirts without ties, whereas account executives will adopt the sober dark suit, white shirt and innocuous tie expected of 'humdrum' office personnel. A client expects creative personnel to act the part and look 'creative'. Their dressed-down attire not only sets them apart from the standardized appearance of those employed in the business world; it helps them work, they say, in a relaxed and free manner.[52] Clients accept this because they do not have to interact with creatives every day. The account executives who are assigned that job, however, dress like those with whom they interact. As Goffman later comments: 'Executives often project an air of competency and general grasp of the situation, blinding themselves and others to the fact that they hold their jobs partly because they look like executives, not because they work like executives.'[53] In this way the account team, or 'performance team',[54] neatly combines through manner and appearance the two requirements sought after by a client in search of an advertising agency: 'creativity' (however it may be defined – a problem taken up in the following chapter) and a business-like approach to everyday matters of importance to the client.

As we saw when I described the opening speeches given by senior managerial staff at the Frontier presentation, purely ceremonial roles are given to certain members on each side and these people are concerned more with the appearance they give off, than with the one that they give. At the same time, since every team member has the power to give the show away or at least to disrupt it by inappropriate behaviour,[55] each enters into a bond of mutual dependency on the other's behaving appropriately. This mutual dependence cuts across hierarchical organization and integrates divisions otherwise established by managerial levels – something already commented on in my discussion of the split-account system.

At the same time, however, precisely because account team members have to co-operate to maintain a front in the presence of their client, they are hardly able to maintain such an impression in one another's company. 'Accomplices in the maintenance of a particular appearance of things, they are forced to define one another as persons "in the know", as persons before whom a particular front cannot be maintained.'[56] Such familiarity was extended to me when I was officially incorporated in the Frontier account team. This privilege of familiarity – what Goffman calls 'an intimacy without warmth'[57] – was not something organic, developing with the amount of time we spent together. Rather, it was a formal relationship that was automatically extended and accepted as soon as I took my place on the team.

In presentations such as the ones I witnessed, participants – especially the person making the pitch – know exactly what they are up to and calculate very precisely how to make an impression by means of language and other readily understood symbols. This is what Goffman refers to as the expression that someone gives. What is less controllable, however, is the impression that a participant gives *off*, through non-verbal cues – like clothing, grooming, gestures, technical support, and so on – that others present can construe as somehow symptomatic of the person, and thus the organization, giving them off. These are much more difficult to control – like Ueda's gradually dishevelled collar and tie, accompanied by beads of perspiration, as he gave his presentation to Frontier – and generally attract the attention of those witnessing the verbal performance. There is thus a 'fundamental asymmetry' in the communication process, since people are generally better equipped to see through another's attempt at calculated unintentionality than they are at manipulating their own behaviour. In short, while the individual concerned *ex*presses himself, those in whose presence he is are *im*pressed and make their judgements largely by inference.[58]

There was a good example of the reading of signs given off during a perform-ance when the Asatsu account team held an impromptu post-mortem meeting in the follow-up to its initial pre-presentation to Frontier staff. Having himself wit-nessed the account team's presentation style and watched carefully the client's reactions, the head of the International Division quickly decided that there should be only one presenter, not three; he also made it clear that the account team had to know *why* it was not going for the client's senior manager's favourite tag line, *The Light of Joy and Creativity*, since those present from Frontier had queried the fact that the agency did not use it in the pre-presentation. On the basis of an overheard *sotto voce* remark about 'prostitution', one of the ad series presented (the Young Women series) was at once discarded, while another (Home Entertainment) was promoted because it illustrated a product sales approach that clearly appealed to Tanaka from Frontier (to judge from the expression on his face when he saw it). In other words, in many ways the most important aspect of this meeting, in strategic terms, was the agency's impression of the client's expressive reaction to, as well as initial impression of, what the account team had originally expressed.

This meeting was a good example of how a team shifts from front to back-stage performance, depending on circumstance. During the pre-presentation to Tanaka and his two colleagues from Frontier, the account team behaved formally and respectfully towards its visitors. They represented the advertising agency, Asatsu, just as Tanaka and his colleagues represented Frontier. The moment the latter had been seen off the premises, however, the account team and senior managerial staff immediately shifted into back- stage informality. They were no longer 'Asatsu', but account manager, media buyer, copywriter, marketing director, and so on – with their different professional expertise and divisional affiliations. This role change was marked by a shift in language register, from polite to plain style of speaking, as well as by the removal of jackets as team members worked once more in shirtsleeves. Their general body language, too, was far more relaxed. A couple of men slouched in chairs, rather than sat upright with straight backs. One man twirled a pencil between his fingers; a second doodled idly on notebook paper; a third cracked his knuckles noisily. These contradictions of impressions given off only a few minutes previously merely reinforced how much the pre-presentation dramaturgical performance had been painstakingly fabricated. A similar situation recurred after the presentation itself when there was some subdued joking, as well as mutual encouragement, among some members of the account team as they packed up their gear in the anteroom to Frontier's presentation room and prepared to leave for a leisurely lunch during which they went over what had gone on during the presentation, and ribbed Ueda for the way in which both his clothing and his speech had seemed to fall apart the longer his pitch went on.

Not surprisingly, a team's entire back region is kept screened off from a potential audience – something that applies both to ad agency *and* to client, so that all I am able to comment on here is what went on in Asatsu, and not in Frontier or the competing agency, J&M. Usually, in Western societies, there are forms of communication (like mimicry, cursing, criticism, caricature) that are carried on back stage which directly contradict front-stage behaviour.[59] Back-stage behaviour in Western societies tends to consist of:

> Reciprocal first-naming, cooperative decision-making, profanity, open sexual remarks, elaborate griping, smoking, rough informal dress, 'sloppy' sitting and standing posture, use of dialect or sub-standard speech, mumbling and shouting, playful aggressivity and 'kidding', inconsiderateness for the other in minor but potentially symbolic acts, minor physical self-involvements such as humming, whistling, chewing, nibbling, belching, and flatulence.[60]

As my description above intimates, Japanese have similar ways of relaxing formality. But there are notable differences. I never heard cursing, mockery, sarcasm, mimicry, satire or caricature, for example; nor did 'minor physical self-involvements' extend to belching or flatulence (although knuckle cracking was a fearsome substitute). Moreover, unlike the situation in Western societies, Japanese tended to adopt standard rules of etiquette and subtly put the audience and not the performers in a favourable light.[61] In this respect, there was a merging between front-stage behaviour and its concern with formality and respect, on the one hand, and back-stage behaviour symbolic of intimacy and disrespect for others present, on the other – supporting Goffman's argument that all behaviour tends to combine both styles.[62]

Conclusion

In this chapter, I have used the case study of Asatsu's preparations for the Frontier presentation to look at various aspects of impression management. One of these was the idea of a presentation as a cultural or dramaturgical performance. Another was to see it as part of a social drama. A third was to follow how self-presentation was enacted at both individual and team levels.

Advertising agencies are in business because they can, they say, create images that will persuade people to buy products and thus link the world of production with that of consumption. They are thus in the business of managing impressions on two fronts. The first is that which affects us in our everyday lives, wherever we live and whatever we do: the advertising campaigns that agencies create for their clients. It is their job to make a particular car, CD player, beer or perfume stand out in such a way that we are persuaded to buy it the next time we visit a supermarket or store. That advertising in this way 'manages' our impressions has led to considerable criticism on the part of journalists, as well as academics in linguistics, semiotics, women's and cultural studies.[63] I do not intend to deal with such criticisms here, primarily because they have been made purely from the point of view of advertising's audience and do not take into account some important issues surrounding the processes of production in the advertising industry – processes which have an inevitable effect on the finished product.[64]

This brings me to the second front on which advertising agencies may be said to manage impressions: one that has been the focus of this chapter. When an agency gives a presentation, it claims a particular expertise and seeks to have that claim honoured by the client.[65] Although that expertise is indeed its ability to come up with creative ideas to sell an advertiser's products and services, as well, occasionally, as the advertiser itself as a corporation (part of the Frontier remit to Asatsu), an advertising agency is generally more concerned to foster an impression on its client that it is a professional, business-like and credible organization with which it can safely conduct its business. On this front, the management of impressions that takes place has virtually nothing to do with the consumers at which the client's advertising campaign is to be directed, and everything to do with the client company itself, and its representatives.

It will be recalled that during the build-up to Asatsu's presentation to Frontier, the account team expressed a lot of concern about Frontier's senior executive and final decision-maker, Oba. What was it that *he* liked and disliked when it came to choice of a tag line? What was *his* take on his company's products and sales strategy in Germany and the United States? Should Asatsu flatter him by choosing *The Light of Joy and Creativity* as its tag line, even though nobody – in particular, the two foreigners assigned to the account team – thought it appropriate? Or should the agency show a bit of independence and come up with its own tag line? And, if it did, how would that affect its position vis-à-vis the rival agency, J&M? What strategy was *it* likely to adopt in the presentation, and how different would it be from Asatsu's?

In short, the agency spent a lot of time positioning itself vis-à-vis both its client and its rival agency, and less time positioning Frontier and its products vis-à-vis targeted consumers, although the latter had, of course, to be taken into account when the account team made its market analysis and accompanying creative strategy. The point here is that, as in many service and creative industries which supply a product for one audience but are paid by another, an advertising agency has to ensure that it manages different kinds of impressions on both supply and demand sides of its business.

In this chapter, as I have said, the discussion has focused entirely on the mutual management of impressions between an agency and its potential client. Here information control has been crucial, as each has tried to ensure that the other cannot, and does not, disrupt the overall performance in any way. Each has aimed 'to sustain the definition of the situation that its performance fosters', by means of an over-communication of some facts and an under-communication of others.[66] In this respect, the keeping of 'dark' (stemming from misrepresentation), 'strategic' and 'inside' secrets becomes very important.[67]

Strategic secrets prevent an audience from effectively adapting to a state of affairs that, in this case, an ad agency is planning to bring about. And yet agency personnel spend a lot of time wheedling strategic secrets out of their audience – witness Oba's likes and dislikes, the competing agency's likely tactics (Asatsu even managed to get hold of one of J&M's prior presentations to Frontier), and so on. As we saw in the previous chapter on advertising talk, certain information may not be strategic at the time it comes into circulation among agency personnel, but may be kept secret because there is a chance that it may acquire strategic importance in the future.[68]

As we have seen in previous chapters, therefore, the trading of information – in particular, of reliable information – is a vital part of an agency's role as communicator between what are essentially two kinds of clients, whose spheres of knowledge about the commodities in which they share an interest overlap very little. This is one technique by which, like its rivals, Asatsu hopes to maximize its performance. It is also in its interest to ensure that these spheres remain separate, which is why Asatsu only hints at 'secrets' it knows about consumers to a manufacturer, and keeps consumers more or less in the dark about why it is conducting certain types of research. Possession of inside secrets marks someone out as being a member of a group and helps that group differentiate itself from other groups. Such inside secrets may very well be both dark and strategic, and consequently exaggerated as insider gossip. The emphasis on secrecy also partly explains why agencies tend to be structured into different divisions that focus exclusively on different aspects of their work – account servicing, creative, marketing, special promotions, media buying, and so on. So, not only does every agency act as bridging mediator between producer and consumer; every account executive acts as mediator within an agency, co-ordinating the work of those members of different divisions who constitute his account team, or 'specialized knowledge group'.

But how much is the agency taken in by its own claims to a professional under-standing of both client and consumer needs? There were times when members of an account team were convinced of the originality of the ideas presented to a client and were sincerely bewildered when their staging of these ideas failed to meet with the client's approval. Often, however, they were not taken in by their own routines and were merely concerned to convince their client as a means to further ends.[69] Such cynicism is fairly common in service occupations where 'practitioners who are otherwise sincere are sometimes forced to delude their customers because their customers show a heartfelt demand for it.'[70]

Preparations for the Frontier presentation showed, I think, the Asatsu account team members struggling to steer a course at least midway between the two poles of a credibility-cynicism continuum. They made an honest attempt to analyse the market in such a way that Frontier and its products would be differentiated from competitors, but ruthlessly exploited inside knowledge of individual tastes in the client's company when it came to deciding which campaign series to advocate. Yet they did not become totally cynical and suggest that Frontier adopt its managing director's favourite tag line. Instead, the account planner went out on a limb by sug-gesting that none of the tag lines provided by the client was appropriate and that a totally new one – *It's in the Name* – would be more suitable. It was this 'original', or at least different, approach that persuaded Frontier to opt for Asatsu, rather than the competing agency, J&M. It *could* be, therefore, that the client was as aware of the potential for underlying cynicism in the performance of apparent credibility as were members of the agency's account team. But I don't know; I wasn't there back-stage in Frontier.

Which brings us to why credibility should be important at all. We have seen that account team members-as-performers operated in both front and back regions during the course of their preparations for a competitive presentation, while the client-as-audience was only present in the front region (and consumers-as-out-siders were excluded from both). Indeed, the agency's success in being seen as a professional, legitimate and credible partner depended in large part on its being able to get into and find out about the closely guarded back region of its audience, the client.

Such tactics are not exclusive to the advertising industry. Every corporation must seem credible in what it does. It must be seen to be professional in its activ-ities, to serve its partners, clients and customers, to be effective in its management, strategic in its planning, sound in its financial administration, and so on. Such cor-porate credibility depends on careful planning back stage within an organization, as well as on the discovery and strategic use of back-stage information in other organizations. In other words, the management of a credible impression is ulti-mately a businessman's and business organization's trick of the trade.

–5–

Creativity and Constraints

Another issue that emerges from the discussion of the agency's preparations for the presentation to Frontier is that of creativity. You will doubtless recall that, during Asatsu's preparations for its presentation to Frontier, the account team found itself in a quandary over several issues connected with its campaign ideas. One of these was which tag line to use. In its orientation, Frontier had provided the competing agencies with three different tag lines: *The Art of Entertainment*, *The Pulse of Entertainment* and *The Light of Joy and Creativity*. Although initially plumping for *The Pulse of Entertainment*, Asatsu's account team was concerned that the senior Frontier executive, Oba, who was probably the man who was going to make the final decision about which agency to hire, was very keen on *The Light of Joy and Creativity*. What would happen if the account team decided to ignore his preference? Would Asatsu fail to win the account as a result? Was there any way around this seeming impasse?

In the end, thanks to my own little intervention, the account manager, Ueda, decided to go for *The Pulse of Entertainment*, but then added a second phrase, *Entertaining Ideas for the Future*, backed up by *Like the Name Says* and *It's in the Name*. It was the fact that Ueda was ready to come up with new tag line ideas, rather than stick to the ones provided by the client, that helped persuade Frontier's decision-makers to give the account to Asatsu. This time, at least, the agency had stuck to its marketing analysis in coming up with creative ideas and had not toadied to the whims of its client.

What is clear, though, is that the preferences of individual client (and, occasionally, agency) personnel can often affect an agency's decision as to what to include in, or exclude from, its creative platform. After all, it is the client who provides the financial wherewithal for an advertising agency to stay in business and thrive. The client, therefore, and not the consumer, tends to get first nod. We saw this in the account team's deliberations over which of its six prepared ad campaigns to propose to Frontier at the presentation proper. The Young Women series was dropped because Tanaka was heard to mutter 'prostitution' to one of his colleagues. The Nature series was adopted, in spite of objections from the two foreigners present in the account team and in spite of the fact that my own unsystematic questioning of foreign friends revealed that two other series were preferred, because Ueda knew that it would appeal to Oba and Tanaka (more of this in the following chapter on representations of the Other).

In this chapter, I want to look at some of the issues involving the organization, ideals and practices of creativity in the face of various conditions or constraints encountered by creative practitioners in the advertising industry. My aim is two-fold: first, to look at what copywriters and art directors have to say about creativity as used in advertisements themselves; and second, to examine creativity in the organizational context of an advertising agency and its relations with the clients who order advertising. In this way, following the example partly set by Thomas Frank,[1] I hope to be able to outline the numerous, often paradoxical, links between creativity, management and the market in Japan.

An advertising agency, as defined by the American Association of Advertising Agencies (AAAA), is 'an independent business, composed of creative and business people, who develop, prepare, and place advertising in media for sellers seeking to find customers for their goods and services'. As the case study will have made clear, advertising is a co-operative venture, usually involving an advertising agency, aimed at transforming basic product data into an expressive form.[2] During this process, an agency needs to subcontract various different individuals and organizations (including freelance photographers, recording studios, model agencies, make-up artists, fashion and hair stylists, video engineers, television production companies, furnishing and set units, and so on) in the preparation of an advertising campaign which it has itself been contracted by a client to create and produce. Because the outcome of a campaign is frequently uncertain (in spite of more or less sophisticated attempts to predict and measure its effect),[3] and because every agency employs both 'creative' and business (or 'humdrum') personnel who bring together a variety of vertically differentiated skills needed to work on a particular project that must be finished within a particular time frame, advertising may be classified – following Richard Caves – as a 'creative industry'.[4]

Although very much like other kinds of industry – farming, shipbuilding and manufacturing in general – advertising differs in that it has to tailor each of its products to individual corporate clients. It produces no concrete, standardized product. Every advertising campaign must necessarily be different from those that have preceded it. As such, it consists of a one-of-a-kind, 'non-material' set of ideas.[5] This has led to the assertion that an advertising agency's 'only stock in trade is creative *ideas*'.[6] But just how these ideas are arrived at remains almost totally unexplored. There is a lacuna in numerous advertising case studies between market analysis of a client's product and the responses generated by a particular creative advertising campaign idea.[7] The fact that we rarely – if ever – get told how an idea happens is a bit like 'the final chapter of a detective story in which the intuitive hero identifies the murderer as the bishop but declines to tell us how he worked it out'.[8]

Because an advertising agency first has to seek clients and then focus its energy on creating a unique advertising campaign for each one in such a way that the latter's product or service is made to appeal to consumers *and* encourage them to buy it, its work is necessarily split into two – not necessarily harmonious – parts. On the one hand, it needs to devote considerable manpower to soliciting, obtaining and maintaining accounts, the sums of money set apart by corporations of all kinds for the advertising of their goods and services. Those employed to this end are the account executives, account managers, and account planners (depending on their exact role, and current management fashions in the advertising business).[9] On the other hand, it also needs to translate its clients' wishes into actual advertising ideas which, in their finished form as print (in newspapers, magazines, posters, bill-boards), broadcast (television and radio commercials), and/or electronic (Internet) advertising, succeed in increasing product sales, improving corporate image, or generally attracting attention. For this purpose, an advertising agency employs 'creative' staff – generally consisting of copywriters, who write the words in ads, and art directors (or ADs) who are trained in graphic design (for print advertising), film (for television commercials) or computers (for Internet advertising).

That 'humdrum' account and 'creative' copy and art personnel do not always get along is a well-remarked fact in the advertising industry,[10] which has, over the years, debated – on occasion vociferously – the relative merits of each group of employees. As Jim Young, of J. Walter Thompson, once noted in his diary of an ad man's life in the Second World War years:

> At lunch today on the Tavern terrace listened again to the perennial debate over the rel-ative importance of creative men and account executives in agencies. The creative men claim too much. A garden must have plenty of fertilizer if plants are to flourish, but even so grasshoppers can do you out of fruit or bloom. Creative men usually supply the chemicals that make accounts grow, but, Lord, how the grasshoppers need to be watched![11]

Part of the problem is historical. The advertising agency came into being when certain entrepreneurs like Volney Palmer (1799–1864)[12] realized that money was to be made from acting as middlemen selling advertising space on behalf of news-papers, which did not have the manpower (or, later, contacts) to do so themselves. The industry – in both the United States and Japan – was thus founded on solici-tation, and it was only some decades after they had initially set up business as space buyers that agencies began to offer customers a new service: preparing copy and artwork on their behalf.[13] At the time, and for some decades afterwards, this extension of service was considered to be an insignificant adjunct of the more important task of soliciting accounts, although nowadays all full service agencies offer their clients a package of services that include creative work, marketing research, media placement and various forms of promotions (from sponsorship of sporting and other events to organizing clients' sales meetings and point-of-purchase (POP) advertising in retail outlets).

The emphasis on obtaining, rather than carrying out, advertising orders is in certain respects paradoxical – rather 'like a doctor working harder to get patients than to cure them'.[14] In short, a greater part of the ongoing creative-humdrum personnel conflict has been financial, although this is not mentioned very much, if at all, in the literature.[15] Since accounts provide the money that enables an agency to employ the people it does employ, as well as enabling those people to maintain families and live the everyday lives they live, there has been a strong feeling within most advertising agencies over the years that those who solicit, obtain and maintain accounts are an agency's lifeline and therefore in some ways superior to those who do not bring in money. Creative personnel are included among the latter because the end result of their work is seen to be the *spending* of a client's money (although copywriters and art directors themselves will counter-argue that it is the creative ideas that they have used in other advertising campaigns that significantly help attract new clients to their agency).

Which argument prevails depends very much on the decisions of senior management. In Asatsu, at least, the super-/sub-ordinate power relations between account managers and creative personnel were sustained by a clear terminological distinction between 'line' and 'staff' employees, on the one hand and, on the other, by corresponding financial differentials in wages and bonuses. It is notable in this respect that, unlike many European and American agencies, Japanese full-service agencies are almost all led by CEOs who come from account management, rather than from the creative side of the business. Although this concurs with standard criticisms of Japanese corporations as management dominated and inflexible, in Asatsu at least, important steps were taken to ensure that the agency's organization and management style were not bureaucratic or inflexible. Indeed, it was generally recognized that, precisely because it produced no standardized product, an advertising agency *must* have flexibility at all levels of its business operations.

One more point should be highlighted with regard to the distinction between creative and humdrum personnel. Because their job is to obtain and manage accounts, account executives tend to focus their attention primarily on the *client* and what the client says it wants, likes, needs, and so on with regard to the advertising campaign it has ordered. In other words, there is a strong tendency for them to 'hold clients' hands'.[16] Creative personnel, however, are more concerned with *consumers*. As hinted at above, advertising presents a client's product or service in a way that enables a reader or viewer to learn what it is and what it promises to do, so that s/he can *evaluate* it critically in the light of other similar products or services. Then, advertising invites that reader or viewer to decide what the product *means* to him/her in his/her everyday life, and then whether it means enough to him/her for it to be really worth *buying*. In other words, copywriters and art directors construct their advertising messages in such a way that ideally everything is left up to the consumer,[17] but their work is paid for by an advertiser who is, for the most part, a producer. It is this inherent potential conflict between accounts and advertisements, money and ideas, producers and consumers, account managers and copywriters and art directors that inspires and constrains the ideas and practices of creativity in all advertising industries throughout the world. The question is: where, when and why do creative personnel get to play first, rather than second, fiddle in their agency's orchestra?

The 'Creative Revolution'

One famous example of when and how creative personnel turned the tables on account men in the United States is to be found in the so-called 'Creative Revolution' led by the agency Doyle Dane Bernbach back in the mid-1960s.[18] At one level this 'revolution' was a way of dealing with perhaps *the* most basic problem in advertising: how to make products that are very similar to one another seem 'unique'. Advertising could only do this, it was argued, by producing visual and linguistic images that were themselves 'unique' – that is, by standing out from the mass of advertisements in some way or other (itself not a particularly novel way of regarding the function of advertising). So long as ads were made along formulaic lines according to 'scientific' principles,[19] creativity was doomed. Agencies needed to adopt a radically different approach to the advertising of their clients' goods and services.

But the Creative Revolution did not just affect the content of the ads themselves. At a second level, it was used by copywriters and artists (now renamed 'art directors')[20] to question the accepted relation between account management and creative work. Creativity, they argued, was being stifled by account men who were more concerned with clients' wishes than with the ads themselves (and therefore with the consumers at whom the ads were aimed). Here the focus of the backlash was on Madison Avenue agencies' traditional bureaucratic and hierarchical management style.[21]

Creativity, in the sense of the more or less mysterious processes by which an ad actually gets made, has always posed a problem for managerial ideology, and the advertising industry seems to go through cycles where one is in control of the other.[22] In the 1950s, when Martin Mayer first wrote about the American advertising industry,[23] the emphasis was still on a rule-guided process involving agency organization (account services), research (marketing), execution of a given idea (creative) and media placement (media buying). In the 1960s, however, everything changed. Tired of what they perceived as organizational constraints on their freedom, up-and-coming young talented copywriters and designers began to set up small 'creative shop' agencies organized along lines very different from the hierarchical management structures that then characterized the old established agencies (like J. Walter Thompson and BBDO). As one agency CEO, Mary Wells, recalled some years later: 'Talent, not organization, was the key to the advertising business ... and the less organization the less interference there was in the truly important creative work.'[24]

The remarkable success of Doyle Dane Bernbach, as well as of several of the 'upstart' creative shops, quickly prompted the established agencies to reorganize themselves into creative units and flat matrix structures as part of their attempt to keep pace. In addition to its effect on ads themselves, therefore,[25] the Creative Revolution initiated a move away from structured towards unstructured, or semi-structured, organizations. As well as emphasizing substance rather than techniques, and claiming that advertising was art, not science, creative personnel were, in the spirit of the age, suspicious of all rules and organizational routines.[26]

But there was a third level in the 'revolution' that needs mentioning here: client defiance. The advertising industry – like many other creative industries – is characterized by what I shall call the *'multiple audience'* property. By this I mean that all advertising is addressed to at least two audiences.[27] On the one hand, there are the advertisers; on the other, targeted consumers. In every agency, therefore, there is a potential clash of interests between account management and creative teams as each seeks to represent what it sees as the interests of the primary constituency it seeks to address.

The emphasis on 'scientific' methods of advertising clearly reflected client, not consumer, attitudes so that one of the effects of the Creative Revolution was a backlash against what creative personnel saw as an obsequious and unnecessary massaging of clients' collective egos. The era of the 1960s abounds in tales of how an agency CEO walked out on a client who questioned his 'creative' ideas, or cut off another's tie if it offended him aesthetically. Suddenly, it seemed, it was the agency and not the client who was in control of an advertising campaign. Indeed, in the spirit of the age, clients came to expect agency creative staff to wear 'creativity' as a badge: to be outspoken to the point of rudeness, to throw tantrums, and to exhibit flamboyant clothing, long hair and beards, jewellery and all the other marks of perceived 'creativity'. As Mary Wells told a copywriter who said he could not possibly attend an impromptu board meeting at Philip Morris because he was wearing a floral shirt and jeans: 'Don't be ridiculous! They expect you to dress like that.'[28] Clothing, emotional outbursts and other forms of irrational behaviour helped – and still help – 'assert and define the creative persona'.[29]

This leads Frank to argue that the Creative Revolution was 'fought out along something resembling class lines'.[30] But we can see that it was not class so much as job description that drove the rebellion (although the employment of each category of agency employee in the United States may have been indirectly related to class). As we have seen, the distinction between account managers, on the one hand and, on the other, copywriters and art directors found in every advertising agency represents a division between 'humdrum' and 'creative' personnel said to characterize the *'nobody knows'* property of creative industries in general.[31] Thus the Creative Revolution enabled a shift in internal relations within an agency, as well as in external relations between agency and client. Creative personnel used the concept of 'creativity' to counter the organizational disadvantages of their being 'staff' who, unlike account executives and other 'line' personnel, did not apparently bring in profits, by claiming – successfully, for a while – that creative work in fact generated business of its own accord. In this way, they established that they, too, were 'professionals' who were worthy of colleagues' respect, and who made a vital and calculable impact on their agency's financial standing. Bill Bernbach's celebrated celebration of 'difference' was in effect no more than market positioning.[32]

If an image of creativity was used to assert the power and status of copywriters and art directors within agency organization, as well as 'to dazzle, outwit, or befuddle audiences as the situation require[d] in order to sell their work to account people and clients alike',[33] it also had an effect on the consumers whom their advertising addressed. As advertising came to be seen as an 'art', and as creative people came to be regarded as 'rebels' against corporate order and general non-conformists, it was *homo ludens* (the consumer) rather than *homo faber* (the producer) who became the hero(ine) of the age. Thus were the Puritan values hitherto upheld by manufacturing clients challenged and temporally defeated by a carnivalesque approach to consumption.

This was not something totally unexpected for advertising had always made use of these two contrasting symbolic elements.[34] But when, as part of this leaning towards the carnivalesque, George Lois claimed that 'the adman must live in perpetual rebellion against whatever is established, accepted, received. He must internalise obsolescence, constantly anticipate the new',[35] we are led to realize two things. First, creativity can never be defined by any single set of characteristics, since the notions of 'perpetual rebellion' and 'obsolescence' require that it be continuously and permanently shifting in character. Secondly, creativity was used as justification for marketing consumerism. It is creative expression that allowed an advertising campaign to come into existence, encourage sales, and so perpetuate the cycle of consumption and production. In this respect, the Creative Revolution was 'fundamentally a market-driven phenomena [*sic*]'.[36] There is little to suggest that things are otherwise today.

The Social Organization of Creativity

I have included this somewhat detailed discussion of a particular era in American, and British, advertising because I think it helps us understand the social organization of a Japanese advertising agency today. Bill Bernbach's idea of a creative team, for example, was imported and established as an organizational principle in Asatsu in 1970, while one of the ways in which the agency sought to overcome the inherent paradox of serving multiple audiences was by establishing a dual organizational structure. On the one hand, it had its functional divisions of Account Services, Marketing, Media Buying, Promotions and so on down to Creative and Personnel. The very order of these divisions in the agency's organizational chart revealed the low status held by the Creative Division (precisely because it spent money – unlike the first four which brought it in). On the other hand, Asatsu's CEO, Masao Inagaki, had done two things to help militate against divisional bureaucracy and hierarchy. Firstly, he introduced the concept of what he called *zen'in keieishugi*, or 'total management' style of decision-making, whereby – you will recall – *any* employee, regardless of his or her position in the company, was allowed as a matter of principle to take on-the-spot decisions with regard to the work in hand, without having to refer to superiors. This greatly facilitated the conduct of everyday business in the agency. Secondly, he established a cross-divisional organizational system of account teams, each of which contained at least one account executive, market analyst, copywriter, art director and media buyer brought together for the sole purpose of working on a client's account. This system of project management effectively circumvented divisional interference in individual employees' work.

This matrix system of agency organization was used to deal with approximately 600 accounts. As an indication of differences here between Japanese and other advertising agencies, Asatsu's much larger American partner at the time employed the same number of creative staff (100 persons) to work on just twenty-three accounts. You will remember that the comparatively large number of accounts handled by agencies in Japan is due to the fact that advertisers almost invariably split their advertising appropriations – by product (range), or media, or a combination of the two. The net results of the split-account system on creativity are various and concern, in one way or another, a dissemination of knowledge.

Firstly, on the plus side, since account teams are not fixed, creative personnel find themselves working with different colleagues in Account Services, Marketing and Media Buying every time they start on a new account. This helps them to develop individual networks within the agency and to get a much better knowledge of the organization's activities as a whole. Although this is not unknown in Western advertising agencies, in Japan having more than one partner is the rule, rather than the exception. Secondly, creative teams themselves are not fixed, although copywriters and art directors may have preferences about who to work with on what. Consequently creative personnel find themselves interacting with quite a lot of their colleagues and can, as a result, learn from the latter's experiences on other accounts.

Thirdly, on the minus side, by splitting their accounts advertisers effectively prevent an agency from developing the kind of unity in conception and execution that an advertising campaign, it believes, should rightly have. Precisely because of this withholding of information on the part of the client, agency personnel need to find out as much as they can, both from the client and from the media in which the client's other advertising campaigns are placed. It is here that the tripartite, colluding adversary structure of the industry becomes very clear, but the client's strategy of wielding power over its agencies in this way effectively strengthens the position of account management vis-à-vis creative staff in Japanese agencies and makes the probability of client interference in creative ideas more likely.

It is perhaps the fact that creative personnel in Japanese agencies do not find themselves assigned to a single account team, in the way that they usually are in American and European agencies, that explains their overall acceptance of, and sympathy with, the different kinds of work conducted by colleagues in different parts of the Agency's business. The sheer variety of both work and co-operation, coupled with a Japanese 'cultural disposition' that favours teamwork over individuality, does not permit most Japanese creative staff working in advertising agencies – certainly not in Asatsu – to fall into the egoistic trap of thinking that they are talented 'geniuses'.[37] Although there were the by now customary sartorial signs of 'creativity' – jewellery, tinted glasses, snazzy clothes – creative staff generally behaved with the kind of decorum expected of salaried employees in Japan. They did not indulge in tantrums or other emotional outbursts of the kind described by Robert Jackall and Janice Hirota.

The ever-present shadow of hundreds of different clients looming over them probably contributes to this mindset. Famous copywriter, Shigesato Itoi warns that it is a big mistake to think of an idea as 'creative' or 'smart' (*oshare*). To understand creative work, he continues, one should also learn about and understand other jobs related to advertising – either in other parts of an advertising agency or by helping out at a local corner shop.[38] Hidehiko Sekizawa, now director of Hahuhodo's research centre, HILL, asserts that copywriting does not differ essentially from design, marketing or account management. All four branches of agency work are involved in what he calls 'intellectual creativity' (*chiteki sōzō*).[39]

This is not to suggest that creative staff in Asatsu did not see themselves as 'creative' vis-à-vis some of their colleagues, especially those in account management. Nor is it to overlook the fact that account executives sometimes expressed the wish that their creative colleagues were *more* creative, although the latter would respond by saying that they might be, if only they were given more time to think about the products they were being asked to advertise, and if only the client and account men did not direct or restrict them so much. In this respect, they criticized the split-account system which they felt did not allow them to do justice to their creative impulses, although they recognized its positive financial implications on the

Agency's financial stability, and therefore their continued employment.[40] Nevertheless, like their American and European counterparts – and against slightly greater odds laid by the split-account system – Japanese copywriters *have* produced memorable campaigns, and they have delighted in playfulness and the carnivalesque – especially in advertising campaigns following Japan's high economic growth in the 1960s and 1970s – to offset the somewhat restrictive Confucian managerial values adhered to by their clients.[41] All in all, therefore, the end results of creativity in Japanese and Western advertising industries do not appear to differ that much.

Conditions for Creativity

So far, I have looked at creativity in the context of social organization. But what is 'creativity' in advertising? Firstly, as a concept, it is comparatively new. The so-called 'creativity crisis' in American business generally seems to have started in the 1950s and, as we have seen, advertising had its own Creative Revolution in the 1960s. Prior to then, those writing about the American advertising industry rarely, if ever, used the word creative. 'Professionalism', yes; 'skills' and 'expertise', yes; 'experience', yes; but not 'creative'.[42] Rather, they described the jobs in hand: preparing copy and illustrations, or artwork.[43] Similarly, the idea of a 'creative industry', as opposed to a 'culture industry' or 'cultural industry',[44] is even more recent.

Secondly, creativity is defined in large part as the ability to go beyond material, social and/or ideological constraints.[45] No creative team starts out with a blank piece of paper and a rough general idea of what it needs to do. It is presented with what is known as a creative 'brief' or orientation, as we saw with the Frontier case – the strategy directing the course a particular campaign is to take, based on a client's orientation.[46] Both copywriters and art directors often yearn for freedom from the constraints of this brief, but it is the constraints found therein that provide 'the stimulus for invention'.[47] Indeed, one Japanese copywriter argues that the more constraints and conditions laid down by a client the better:

> Occasionally you get asked by a client 'to make something interesting – it doesn't matter what'. Although this kind of request contains virtually no constraints or conditions of any kind, it really causes a lot of problems. I mean, you get totally tied down in trying to work out an advertising angle based on what the word 'interesting' might mean to the client. On the other hand, if a client lays down certain restrictions, what's 'interesting' becomes really clear. In other words, constraints and conditions are a 'fence' that surrounds you ... It is by being surrounded by this fence of constraints and conditions, and by agonising over how to resolve them, that ideas unexpectedly jump out.[48]

Thirdly, the various activities of conception, execution, rationale, support work and client reaction are all constrained to one degree or another by the fact that the production of advertising is a joint activity involving a large number of people,[49] and thus consists of 'networks of people cooperating'.[50] All those concerned need to be able to recognize that 'there are some rules to the game they are playing',[51] so that conventions become extremely important to successful completion of a campaign. In this respect, we should probably turn the idea of 'artistic creativity'[52] on its head. Instead of pursuing questions pertaining to 'criteria of creativity',[53] we should ask: how do constraints give rise to the idea of creativity? In answer, I will here look at six different sets of conditions as they influence creative work in advertising: material, temporal, physical, social, ideological and economic.

Material Conditions

Let us start by examining material conditions. All creative personnel work with standard equipment and materials which affect the way they work and the finished form of that work. They rely on established conventions about how a campaign should be produced in order to go about their work. These conventions dictate what materials will be used; what abstractions are best suited to convey ideas or experiences; and the form in which materials and abstractions are combined.[54] Art directors use a grid system of illustration and copy layout; photographers use different camera lenses, apertures, film, and so on to obtain different effects of light, mass and perspective; copywriters use particular forms of punctuation and type for headlines; commercial directors use freeze frames, soft focus, background music and other conventions developed in film.

The introduction of new technology can change these conventions. With the arrival and common use of computers and digital photography, for example, radical alterations of images are now common in advertisements. Faces are contorted, bodies twisted, limbs elongated. Stray wisps of hair can be removed from, or a beauty spot inserted on, a model's face with a few clicks of a mouse. Airbrushing is the norm, rather than the exception. Digital technology provides art directors, photographers and cameramen with new ways, and new conventions, to carry out their work.

Another material condition is provided by the product. The aim of advertising in Japan is to sell a particular product (as well as to give a favourable impression of a particular corporation).[55] However, there is a world of difference in products, not just in those produced by different companies (like a whiskey or a systems kitchen, for example), but also in those marketed by the same company (like a $4 a bottle downmarket whiskey called Torys, for example, and an up-market expensive brand like Royal, both distilled by Suntory). This makes the nature of the ads created for each product entirely different.[56]

Some products – like foods and beverages – are made to be consumed fairly rapidly, to enable repeat purchases by consumers. These are known as 'staples'. Others – like those connected with household interior (dining tables, sofas, beds, and so on) – are made to last and are therefore regarded by most consumers as 'one-off' or 'single-item' purchases. Yet others – clothing and automobiles are classic examples – appear to be made to last, but are in fact subject to stylistic or technological obsolescence, so that consumers find themselves buying them fairly regularly, even though there may be no 'inherent' need to do so. Besides the functions they perform, products are likely to attract or repel consumers because of a particular combination of audial, visual, tactile, olfactory and/or taste properties with which they are imbued. Any one or more of these may be picked out as a way of advertising the product as a whole: for example, 'At 60 miles an hour the loudest noise in the new Rolls Royce comes from the electric clock',[57] or 'Meisaku wa, mazu kaori tatsu' ('Famous creations, start with fragrance') (Suntory Reserve whiskey).

The product, therefore, conditions the direction in which creative expression will go – whether it will tend to simplicity and economy of expression; adopt a quiet and persuasive or light-hearted style; develop an emotional, rather than rational, personality for the product; make a particular kind of claim; or use a reason-why approach in any one advertisement.[58] The product is always the key to an advertising campaign story,[59] even though it may be a service linked to the product, rather than the product itself, that is advertised.[60]

Those working in the advertising industry will also point to the basic information as a condition for the development of product advertising.[61] Information forms the crux of advertising.[62] Everyone, from account managers to media buyers, needs to know exactly what the product is, how it is made, what it does, who it is for, how long it is supposed to last, how it compares with and differs from competing products, and so on and so forth. Copywriters, in particular, say that they need to read, mark, learn and inwardly digest this information as a fundamental step in the process of coming up with a creative idea or strategy.

Such information is not necessarily limited to the written word, as Claude Hopkins discovered when working on an advertising campaign for Schlitz Beer back in the early decades of the nineteenth century.[63] By talking to people employed in the brewery, he came to realize that his informants did not see that methods which they regarded as ordinary were extraordinary to those who had no understanding of the processes of making beer – an observation echoed many years later by a fellow American, Leo Burnett: 'Golden selling ideas and pungent, persuasive phrases often fall from the lips of users, salesmen – yes, and even clients themselves, to say nothing of their engineers, factory superintendents and other production people.'[64]

Finally, *media* act as a material constraint. Which medium is used for an advertising campaign often depends on the product advertised, but it will ultimately affect its overall style. For example, a product like a contact lens, because of its 'medical' characteristics, often needs to include a lot of information. Thus, illustrated brochures with adequate explanatory text will be written for point-of-purchase retail outlets, while ads with photo and more limited body copy will be placed in magazines read by its target market (young women aged between nineteen and twenty-seven years). Television will be used but sparingly, the prime purpose of commercials being to attract attention to the new product's existence.[65] An advertisement for a department store sale, on the other hand, will be placed in newspapers alone because they provide space for information, and enable exact timing of a campaign thanks to their twice-daily publication. With another product, such as a whiskey, the focus may be more on television commercials as the preferred medium of advertising, because its manufacturer wishes to put across a certain emotional mood suggested by the way the liquid is poured into a glass, as well as by the product's colour, presumed distinctive flavour, smell and effect.

Temporal Conditions

A second set of conditions surround the use of *time* in advertising. Precisely because a campaign has to be finished by a particular date to coincide with a client's production, distribution or other marketing activities, the advertising industry is characterized by a *time flies* property.

Time is important, firstly, in the sense of *when* a product or service is to be advertised, and how this affects both production and media. Timing is often of great importance in advertising since marketing is marked by important cyclical and one-off events. If a new car is to be launched on 1 September, for example, or chocolates prepared in time for Valentine's Day, an advertising campaign must not only be prepared and ready to be sent to selected media at least one month before the date in question, those media must have been persuaded to run the ads or commercials at the right time, and not three days after the event has passed.

Time is also a conditioning factor in broadcast advertising. The length of time given over to a television or radio advertisement necessarily affects its content. A fifteen-second television commercial, for example, offers extremely limited opportunity for an advertiser to include very much more than its own name and the name of the product or service it is promoting, whereas a one-minute radio commercial enables a fast-talking narrator to give information about a product and even to repeat catchy sell-lines. The shorter the time available to broadcast advertising, the more likely it is to rely on 'mood' rather than 'information' as its mode of persuasion.

Third, time is important in its long-term effect on the production of advertising generally. All advertising campaigns should, ideally, be different from previous campaigns, both from campaigns for the product being advertised and from those of competing products, in order to mark them off as 'significant'. At the same time, ideally, they should be distinct from other advertising currently placed in the selected medium. As Ralph Hower noted some decades ago: 'One of the major problems of the art director is to obtain layouts and art work which not only make an advertisement attractive in itself, but also give it strong individuality when it appears beside competing advertisements.'[66]

Every advertising campaign should also, ideally, fulfil a double function – surpassing what has already been achieved, formally realized and technically solved, while simultaneously maintaining everything that is capable of solving a marketing problem. In this respect, like artistic creation, every campaign, again ideally, 'takes apart the structure which was formerly created but restores it in a more complex form and gives to its components a new meaning, a new value, and a new structural role in the totality of the work'.[67] Thus temporal, in the sense of historical, constraints permit the advertising industry to continue in the spiralling quest for 'difference' that characterizes the 'free market' economy.

Physical Conditions

In Asatsu, those involved in the creative process sometimes divorced themselves from the mundane routine of everyday life, to focus exclusively on preparing campaign ideas. This was particularly the case when the agency was involved in preparations for an important client presentation. This separation takes three forms. It is physical, in the sense that creative personnel often worked in a room especially set aside for the duration of the presentation, although normally they would be located at their desks in the Creative Division's building. This physical separation is characteristic of organization in other advertising agencies, both in Japan and elsewhere.[68] Umeki Susumu, for example, comments on how all apprentice copywriters at Hakuhodo were placed together in a separate 'research centre' while learning their trade, and only later were assigned to working in the agency's offices. He also relates that he often shuts himself up in a hotel room when writing copy – mainly because he does not want his colleagues to see how haggard and red-eyed he gets when struggling with copy ideas for a campaign.[69]

In many ways, this physical separation is also ritualistic. Creative people are expected to isolate themselves in one way or another while preparing for a presentation. But the presentation itself has its ritual aspect, as I noted in an earlier chapter. As a 'tournament of value', it takes place in a special room, not normally used in everyday business affairs, and is often secluded in its view. It is thus set apart in terms of place, time, setting and props.

The physical separation is also contractual, in the sense that standard work hours often do not apply, and creative personnel in an agency work well into the early hours of the morning, night after night (and so are entitled to come in late the following morning), as well as through weekends. At the same time, however, these periods of sustained activity are also occasions when creative staff are provided with the opportunity, and burdened with the expectation, to show off the skills that have led to their being employed by the agency in the first place.

Social Conditions

Social conditions of creativity may be broadly distinguished into three sub-sets: those stemming from the fact that the production of advertising consists of close co-operation among 'networks of people cooperating'; [70] those arising because every campaign idea has to be approved by the client prior to its execution; and those that affect the content of the advertisements themselves.

First, let us look at social conditions *within* the organization in which creative personnel work. Whenever Asatsu is asked to work on a client's account, it immediately forms an account team consisting of account manager, and possibly one or two other account executives, marketing team, media planner(s) and creative team (consisting of copywriter and art director, plus – if warranted – television director, under the leadership of a creative director). It is this team which forms the kernel of the 'motley crew',[71] and which works together to create an advertising campaign.[72]

It is the partnership of copywriter and art director that is crucial to the account team's overall endeavour. Following the client's orientation, an account team will have one or two 'brainstorming' sessions, followed by an 'incubation period' during which the creative team usually spends some days thinking and toying with ideas. 'Partners "bounce ideas around" or "play ideas off" each other in a spontaneous, free-association way.'[73] They often swap their established roles, so that the copywriter will suggest visual details and the art director (AD) copy ideas. They will also raid other art forms – like photography, poetry and film – as part of what is in effect a careful planning process, as intuitive ideas are subjected to reasoned critique to see whether they would hold up in practice and so be acceptable to a client. Other account team members will participate in this process, and there may well be strongly held differences of opinion between account executives and the marketing team, on the one side of an argument, and the creative team on the other. Nevertheless, all concerned often introduce periods of relaxation and joking exchanges in meetings and so cease creative activity per se. During this time they may ridicule, caricature or satirize anything and anyone from product and client to celebrities and other public figures who might be used in the campaign.[74] As time passes, the account team agrees on a creative strategy and the copywriter's and AD's work tends to take on a certain momentum of its own and be executed extremely quickly. This has been called the 'takeover effect'.[75]

The second set of conditions concerns relations *between* advertising agency and its client, the user. As noted earlier, it is the client who lays out certain conditions that must be fulfilled in an advertising campaign. When these conditions are related to its product in one way or another, an agency makes sure that they are followed to the letter. But there are times when the client interferes with work prepared by the creative team by insisting on an over-prominent display of its name or logo, for example, or conservative clothing for a supposedly trendy celebrity endorsing its product, or a change in a particular colour used by the AD. Here, all kinds of social conditions are at work, ranging from personal taste (regarding colour) to corporate image (celebrity clothing), by way of organizational politics (name and logo). Such 'sops to vanity'[76] bring into question the initial hiring of the creative team,[77] and stretch its combined patience.

To get round this problem, most creative staff point to the necessity of getting close to clients, even though this is formally an account management task. Sekizawa Hidehiko, for example, stresses that both account executive and copywriters are involved in the same task of breaking down the 'prison walls' surrounding both clients and consumers and in getting close to them in order to 'touch their unconscious' (*muishiki no bubun*).[78]

Precisely because of the indeterminate nature of the elements (people, colour, voice, sound) that go into, for example, a television commercial, and because of the uncertainty surrounding the final result (what Caves calls the *Nobody knows* property), creative people have to build up relations of *trust*. Trust in fact becomes the deciding factor in the production of advertising,[79] and needs to exist at three different levels of organizational interaction. In the first place, because they are both hemmed in by constraints of one sort or another, but particularly by those stemming from the client, copywriter and AD have to trust each other to be able to work together effectively. Secondly, trust must exist between ordinary creative and other personnel, including both account executives and more senior managers, within an agency, so that copywriter and AD can get on with their job without interference. Thirdly, trust has to be built up through interaction between agency and client.[80]

There are two aspects to such relations. On the one hand, creative people should be able to meet a client organization's top management (although their own agency's organizational constraints often prevent this), in order to be able to understand clearly the problems that need to be addressed in a campaign.[81] On the other, socializing of any kind with clients establishes trust and trust enables ideas to be put into effect.[82] As Leo Burnett succinctly put it: 'The simple fact is that the better people know you the better they will like you and the more likely they will be to accept your proposition.'[83] In short, trust is seen as a way of overcoming some of the organizational weaknesses in advertising, and other creative industries induced by the *nobody knows, art for art's sake, motley crew, time flies, A list/B list,* and *infinite variety* properties laid out by Richard Caves.

The third set of social conditions affecting creative output is the effect of personal likes and dislikes on what is, or is not, accepted in an advertising campaign.[84] Often enough, it is the taste of someone on the client side – very often, a senior decision-making manager – that needs to be taken into account by an agency when preparing copy, putting together images, or selecting a celebrity endorser (and, as we saw above, the clothes and make-up that s/he will wear). If an important decision-maker on the client side reveals a favourable impression of a particular campaign idea, an agency's creative team will often go for it, regardless of whether or not that idea is best for the consumers targeted. Needless to say, this does not often make for either 'creative' or effective advertising in terms of sales.

But likes and dislikes can also affect creative work *within* an agency, although this was not an issue that I came across in Asatsu. According to Jackall and Hirota:

> Account subordinates often veto ideas that creatives consider promising for fear their superiors may dislike them. Sometimes the same process works in reverse. Account subordinates think their superiors will like an idea and ask creatives to work at expanding it; but, when the idea is presented to higher-ups, it is unceremoniously tossed out.[85]

Ideological Conditions

Creative staff work in a climate of approval of their endeavours. Generally speaking, there was a tacit acceptance in Asatsu that creative teams were the ones who came up with headlines and visual images that brought market research and analysis to life. This acceptance on the part of other members of an account team included the attitude that creative personnel should be free, to some extent at least, to juggle ideas that came to them and that seemed most appropriate to the campaign being developed. For their part, copywriters and art directors tended to see themselves as competing with themselves to come up with better ideas than they had produced for previous presentations and ad campaigns. They thus expressed themselves through their work, although they readily recognize inputs from others in their account team.

Ideological conditions are primarily 'aesthetic'. In Asatsu, the main aim of creative work was to discover a story or 'talking point' (*kadai*) as part of a campaign's attempt to get people to buy a client's product. Such talking points were usually discovered initially through market research. The creative team's task was to transform that research into a total image by means of copy, visual style, celebrity, music and so on; to position its advertising campaign just half a pace ahead of society; and to make people *want* to catch up with what they perceived to be going on. It was precisely this 'half pace' that was extremely difficult to gauge. If a campaign failed to move far enough forward or, alternatively, moved too far out on a limb, nobody would pay any attention to it. At the same time, though, it was equally difficult to maintain a lead of just half a pace, because competitors were always striving to catch up and then gain an edge by creating their own talking points. This explained the need for new advertising campaigns and for the continual development of the industry as a whole.[86]

Creative staff also added that, precisely because they were aiming to place their clients' products only half a pace ahead that ultimately there was no such thing as originality in their work. Rather, there was merely 'bricolage' (*kumiawase*) where people worked within the conventions of a 'style' and only shifted its boundaries very gently, a little at a time. This militated against any idea of 'individuality' (*kosei*) or a single person's creativity in the production of advertising campaigns – an ideological condition that neatly accorded with Japanese teamwork (*shūdan-shugi*) in general.

Another focus of ideological attention was the relation between what may loosely be termed 'inspiration' and 'thought'. Most creative personnel seem to be agreed that advertising is a commercial art form that results from a combination of 'reason, emotion and hunch';[87] 'inspiration (*omoitsuki*), study (*benkyō*) and sheer hard work (*doryoku*);'[88] not a 'sudden flash of inspiration' (*futto omou*) so much as craftsmanship (*kōfu*) and hard work.[89] As Jim Young puts it: 'Inspiration and flair are great qualities in this business, but for real results give me the man who never quits trying.'[90]

My own research in Asatsu supports these attitudes. Creative personnel suggested that there was no 'set of rules' (*hōhōron*) that could be followed every time a copywriter or art director sat down to dream up ideas.[91] This in itself may be seen as a 'rule' of some sort, however, so that Burnett's hypothesis that what is needed is *'conditioned intuition*, which is a composite of judgment, experience, a God-given sense of timing, and sheer inspiration', leading to a *'moment of fortunate lucidity'*,[92] is one way of bringing together inspiration and rational thought. What all my informants stressed, however, was that both were needed and that every intuition had to be subjected to rigorous reasoned criticism to see whether the idea would stand up.[93]

What come out of this ideological clash of creativity and constraints are *ideas*. Ideas may refer to anything from a headline or commercial technique to campaign theme, but for Leo Burnett:

> A real Idea has a power of its own and a life of its own. It goes beyond ads and campaigns. Properly employed it is often the secret of capturing the imagination of great masses of people and winning 'the battle of the uncommitted mind' which is what our business is really about.[94]

Advertising sells ideas, but only as 'translated into concrete things and services',[95] which is probably why one copywriter prefers to distinguish between ideas, which are 'tests of feelings', and concepts, which 'can be tested in reality'.[96] The distinction is important, as Robert Jackall and Janice Hirota explain:

Sooner or later one of the partners voices or sketches out an idea that 'takes off', and the team subjects this to a more tempered, searching critique. If the idea survives, it is altered and refined until it becomes a 'concept', that is, a guiding theme symbolically linking the product to the perceived needs or longings of the targeted market audience.[97]

However they may be defined, ideas incorporate a dialectical relationship between reason and emotion, so that it is often hinted that they include an element that is beyond rational control.[98]

Economic Conditions

As you will recall from an earlier chapter, the first and foremost economic condition is that the general state of a country's economy will strongly influence the extent to which advertising agencies may or may not be creative. The Creative Revolution of the 1960s was made possible by a strong economy; it was pushed aside by the recession following the oil shocks of the 1970s. Similarly Japanese advertising flourished in the late 1970s and 1980s, only to fade as the country slipped into a prolonged period of no, and once or twice negative, growth. In times of prosperity, advertisers are prepared to give creative ideas a chance; in times of hardship, they focus on sales and are not prepared to take risks on 'creativity'.

Second, the *budget* put aside by the client for an advertising campaign has a huge effect on its form. The budget determines which media can be used and how frequently. This in itself affects the style and expression adopted in a campaign. In general, the advertising rates of media vary according to a combination of the quantity and quality of the audiences they reach. A mass medium like television, for example, is extremely costly during what are called 'prime time' evening programmes when audiences tend to be gathered round the family or household TV set. It is for this reason that commercials are usually very short, and therefore affected stylistically by the material condition of time (discussed above). Narrowly targeted hobby magazines, on the other hand, are comparatively cheap because of limited circulations, although they have the advantage of clearly defined readerships. An upmarket fashion magazine like *Vogue*, however, may charge considerably more for advertising in its pages than competing fashion magazine titles like *Elle* or *Marie Claire* because, unlike – or not quite like – the others, it can claim a well-heeled, financially well-off, and status-conscious middle-aged readership. Advertisers are also required to submit ads that meet the magazine's 'aesthetic standards'.

Furthermore, the budget influences an advertising campaign's content in another way than that brought on by choice of media (see above). A large appropriation on the client's part enables selection of a foreign (usually exotic), as opposed to domestic, location for filming; a small appropriation may mean that advertising creativity must function within a studio frame. Similarly a big budget may encourage the contracting of a famous international, as opposed to well-known local, star to endorse the client's product. This in itself is likely to affect a campaign's reach and recall.[99] When a client has very little money to spend, creative personnel may seek other means to attract attention to the campaign and make an ad 'take a walk on its own' – for example, by including a bath scene with a well-endowed sixty-year-old actress to attract media comment and speculation about breast implants, or by commissioning a theme song with the same title as the campaign, to be sung by a famous pop star who needs the hit to be included in an annual prestigious New Year's Eve television song contest.[100] In each case, the client's limited budget is used in such a way that the advertising campaign gets free media coverage and remains in the public eye. The aim is to induce what Leo Burnett called 'mind share': 'an instinctive, emotional and spontaneous expression of a predisposition to buy a certain brand'.[101]

Concluding Comment

At the beginning of this chapter, I posed four questions. The first two of these concerned the effects of conditioning and organizational factors on creative practices in the advertising industry. In answer, I have argued that there are two aspects of creativity to be taken into account. One is that found in advertisements themselves, and I have outlined the various material, temporal, physical, social, ideological and economic conditions for creativity in the preparation of copy and artwork. The other is connected with the social organization of an advertising agency. Here I focused on the so-called Creative Revolution in the United States during the 1960s, and showed how the ideas generated by creative personnel at this time instigated major structural changes that not only affected the overall organizational hierarchy of large advertising agencies, but also relations between creative 'staff' and account managing 'line' personnel. I then outlined the structure of a Japanese advertising agency to show how its organization was designed to integrate employees with different functions, and to enable a strengthening of networks and circulation of knowledge and experience, as a result of the split-account system of allocating advertising appropriations by the agency's clients. But I also pointed out how the split-account system obliged account managers to pay particular attention to client needs, so that creative staff found themselves rather more subject to organizational constraints and less able to exercise untrammelled imagination in the execution of their work than are, perhaps, their counterparts in American and European agencies.

The third and fourth questions focused on whether there might be substantial differences in the ways creative people work in the Japanese, British and American advertising industries. Here, the answers are less clear cut. In some respects, like creatives' professional attitudes towards how to come up with creative ideas, copywriters and art directors all over the world seem to share a common vision of their work processes. These apply not just to qualitative, but to quantitative, evaluations, too. For instance, the Japanese copywriter, Susumu Umeki, states that fifty ideas are needed before one ad can be made. Research by a business consultant in the US shows that sixty ideas are needed for one successful innovation.[102]

Creative ideas are the raw material and innovations are the ultimate result. One needs many ideas before one can identify the one which deserves to be implemented and commercialised. Ideas can be generated internally or acquired from the external environment but one thing is clear: one needs many ideas before the idea with the winning streak is found.[103]

In other respects, an organizational difference – such as the split-account system by which advertising appropriations are distributed among agencies in the Japanese advertising industry – influences, on the negative side, the extent to which 'creativity' as a concept is acceptable (because of more likely client interference) and, on the positive side, learning and knowledge processes among creative staff within an agency. This does not mean, however, that the introduction of *zen'in keieishugi* and the establishment of divisional account teams *necessarily* gave rise to creativity in the work of Asatsu's creative personnel, although the free exchange of information and ideas definitely helped create 'a climate of creativity'. Moreover, as in other businesses in other parts of the world, external sources, including competitors, customers, marketing institutions and advertising agencies, are an extremely important source of creative ideas for an organization. By obliging agencies to seek information about its clients' intentions externally – in particular, among media organizations – the split-account system can be said to foster creative approaches to advertising and marketing issues.

Such organizational differences may well be supported by national cultural differences, although to emphasize one over the other is likely to lead to futile chicken-and-egg discussion and theorizing. It so happens that the split-account system works very well for a people who tend to pride themselves on their teamwork and believe in continuous employment rather than hiring and firing according to changing economic conditions in a business. On the other hand, the competing account system appears rather apt for peoples who like to think of themselves as 'free individuals' made or broken by their own efforts, and who link their own personal 'originality' with that of their creative work.

Ultimately, however, creativity exists only because of the constraints present in any creative industry. Such conditions are necessary because they provide those working in the creative industries with reasons or excuses for things not going as planned. For instance, if an advertising campaign fails to sell the product advertised, then various features of the advertising industry can be evoked to 'explain' this failure: either the client was too stringent in its demands; or timing meant that the wrong celebrity or a different photographer was selected from the one the creative team had hoped for (motley crew and A/B list); or the budget put aside for the task was hopelessly inadequate; or ... or ... or ... Creativity is thus an excuse, an ultimate recourse to immeasurable quality-that-might-have-been-if-only this or that.

–6–

In Search of the Other

One thing that has emerged in earlier chapters of this book is that advertising is never quite what it appears to be on the surface. Ad campaigns are, initially at least, addressed to clients rather than consumers. Moreover, the creative ideas adopted by an agency's account team in its presentation are often specifically tailored to the personal whims of particular personnel in the client company. Although the presentation itself seems objectively to be one in which Agency A pitches a few ideas to Client B on the basis of a marketing brief, this business organizational front is actively fabricated by certain individuals on each side who relay back-stage information to one another during preparations for the presentation. This comes about because, for one reason or another – very often arising from an individual's need to take advantage of internal politics within his corporation – all those concerned have a vested interested in ensuring that this particular agency wins this particular account from this particular client at – as politicians are wont to say – this particular point in time.

In order to manipulate appearances successfully, agency and client employees need to have a strategic grasp of what is going on in the other's organization. This is particularly the case with agency personnel whose only product bordering on the concrete is the ideas that go into an ad campaign and who, as a result, need to persuade a would-be client not just of its need to advertise in the first place, but of its wisdom in appointing *their* ad agency to carry out the job in hand. Failure to achieve these aims over an unspecified length of time will ultimately end in their agency going out of business and their losing their jobs.

As part of this process of managing impressions in front of its clients, an advertising agency has to ensure that the advertising and other promotional activities that it conducts on behalf of a client also eventually meet with the approval of targeted consumers, who are induced as a result to buy the product being advertised. Although this in itself is difficult enough, advertising personnel quite often find themselves obliged to address more than one target audience in a single campaign. One of the things that Frontier wanted Asatsu to do, for instance, was not just produce a campaign that would attract a certain type of up-market consumer. It also had to make that campaign idea appeal to those working in Frontier's offices abroad and so encourage them to feel proud of being members of such an important

Japanese company. In a contact lens campaign that I have described elsewhere,[1] the creative team was asked to come up with a campaign that would appeal not just to the 18- to 27-year-old women targeted as primary buyers of the lenses, but also to middle-aged male opticians who would be recommending the lenses to their customers in the first place.

What all this points to is the importance of an understanding of 'the other' in the advertising industry, and it is here – as well as in other pragmatic aspects of research practice – that advertising, marketing and ethnography find themselves in close alignment.[2] Just as anthropologists in the field need to find out about, analyse and explain a foreign 'other' to people back home in order to justify their employment in academic, overseas development, government and business organizations of one sort or another, so do marketers need to learn about consumers and convey the knowledge gained back to clients in such a way that the latter will readily approve their agency's campaign ideas.[3]

Who these 'others' are exactly tends to vary according to circumstance, although agency personnel always find themselves having to deal with client and consumer others. In the case of preparations for the Frontier presentation, the Asatsu account team also had to try to work out the difference – if any – between a German and American other. How would someone in Germany or the United States react to this visual idea or that tag line? And then, would key Japanese personnel in Frontier itself react to the same idea or tag line in an identical manner? In other words, did *they* see German and American others in the same way that the agency's account team did? And what about the two foreigners who were part of that team? How did their views of the Japanese other presented in one or two of the visual series prepared for the presentation mesh with those of their Japanese colleagues? It is questions of this nature that I will address in this chapter.

Orientalism and Occidentalism

Discussions of the other often begin with Edward Said's work, *Orientalism*, in which the Palestinian-born intellectual historian traced the ways in which European scholars writing about the Arab world over the centuries consistently portrayed 'Orientals' by means of various clichés which 'promoted the difference between the familiar (Europe, the West, "us") and the strange (the Orient, East, "them")'.[4] Whereas Europe encouraged individuality, egalitarianism, rationality, and so on, in the Orient collectivism, hierarchy and an emotional approach prevailed. These stereotypes consisted of a number of different strands that, among other things, characterized Oriental women, for example, as exotic, sultry, sensual beings and men as lecherous, cunning and prone to extreme cruelty. Said's general argument was that what he called 'Orientalism' was simultaneously an area studies academic tradition, a style of thought for imagining the Orient, and a corporate institution for 'dominating, structuring, and having authority over the Orient'.[5] As such it has had 'a special place in European Western experience', while 'the Orient has helped to define Europe (or the West) as its contrasting image, idea, personality, experience.'[6]

Although Said was primarily concerned with the Middle East, what he had to say was – and, alas, often still is – in large part valid for other parts of Asia, in particular China and Japan. Anyone with but a passing interest in Japan, I am sure, will be aware of tales of the exotic beauty of the *geisha* and the seeming cruelty, as well as inner spirituality, of the *samurai* (whose purported code of practice, known as *bushidō*, is often referred to with wide-eyed adulation in the business press). The strange love-hate relationship based on admiration and fear that Europeans and Americans exhibit towards the Japanese is characteristic of that which they show towards Arab people. All in all, we may conclude that the discourse about Japan and the West, like the discourse about the Orient and the Occident in general, is a relationship of power, domination and various degrees of hegemony.

Although Said's critique has itself been criticized and an extensive literature has since ballooned over just how we should and do represent the other, I want here to look at ways in which Japanese – especially those past masters of representation, advertising employees – imagine the Occident. Generally speaking, Japanese distinguish between themselves and other Asians (extending as far as India and the South Asian continent); between themselves and Africans; and between themselves and what they call 'the West' (*seiyō*). They also make less general classificatory distinctions between the 'middle east' (*chūkintō*), 'Europe' (*yōroppa*), the United States (*beikoku*), South America (*nanbei*), and so on, but the (predominantly white) people who live there – with the exception of indigenous populations such as American indians and the Inuit – are categorized as 'Westerners' (*seiyōjin*). In other words, in this respect they promote the same sort of difference between 'us' (the familiar) and 'them' (the strange) that Edward Said has noted of Westerners writing about the East (and quoted above).

The kind of essentialism and absolutism adopted by Westerners towards the Orient is also practised by Japanese academics, journalists and businessmen who, like Western authors writing about Japan, define what is notable about the other by resorting to contrasts: for example, individuality versus collectivism, egalitarianism versus hierarchy, discord versus harmony and rationality versus emotions. But, whereas in traditional Orientalist writings, the Oriental is always denigrated for not being individualistic, rational and so on, in Japanese writings, the opposite is true. During the heady days when Japan's economy was booming and Japanese corporations were expanding their operations successfully throughout the Western world, it was phrases like 'teamwork', 'corporate spirit', 'non-verbal communication', even 'culture', that were used to 'explain' Japanese success. In other words, precisely because of their economic success in the second half of the twentieth century, the Japanese were able to recharge negative images previously applied to them by Western Orientalists and successfully propagated a form of 'counter-Orientalism' as a new hegemonic discourse.[7]

An important point to note about the continued efficacy of Orientalist and counter-Orientalist images is that it is the *media* which have been most active in their dissemination to *mass* audiences. In other words, media provide people all over the world with immediate access to stereotype images of the other – images to which people react in all sorts of different ways, without necessarily thinking too deeply about their origins or validity. In this respect, media have, perhaps, far greater influence than ever was exerted by the scholars and administrators discussed by Said in his exposition of Orientalist practices in earlier times.

Part of the reason for the media's adoption of these grossly contorted views of the other is to be found in the constraints of time and/or space under which they operate. The average television news story, for example, does not usually last longer than a few minutes, while most newspaper articles are limited to so many words or columns of a page. So, too, with radio programmes and magazines. As a result, when trying to describe and explain (there is not time to analyse) everything that is going on in the world, different media tend to dish up all-too-similar mouthfuls of exotic bites that are then consumed by their fast-chewing audiences.

Clearly, advertising also suffers from such constraints. A television commercial usually lasts no more than thirty seconds (half that is the norm in Japan), and a radio commercial less than a minute. Each medium therefore constrains what can and cannot be said, and television demands the use of images over information. A half-page newspaper ad or full magazine page ad also limits the amount of information that can sensibly be included therein, but is sufficient to make visual images slightly – though only slightly – less important. The same is true of all other print and digital media. Yet advertising needs to get across a particular set of images that reflect a marketing need and appeal to a particular targeted group of people in a single printed page, television commercial, billboard, digital screen, or whatever.

To this end, those working in the advertising industry have little choice *but* to make use of existing classifications that are readily understood by their targeted audiences. At the same time, they need to ensure that these classifications set the products they are advertising *apart* from other similar products. They are thus likely to avail themselves of existing Orientalist or Occidentalist images in order to achieve their aims, since they do not have the space or time for complicated, or for complicating, issues. In this respect, we may say that at one level the relentless dichotomy of Orientalist and Occidentalist images found in advertising indicates *stylistic* differences – which are compatible and comparable, rather than opposite and irreconcilable.[8] At a second level these common differences are not suppressed but *promoted* and *structured* by an advertising system that is now becoming global in its forms.[9]

As we saw, in preparing for the Frontier presentation, the Asatsu account team adopted as stylistic differences the general structural principles by which Japanese classify foreigners. Americans and Germans were both 'Westerners' (in other words, not 'Japanese') and therefore more or less the same. If pressed, those concerned could fall back on secondary clichés. Americans were only interested in a 'hard sell' (hence the account team's preference for the Entertainment series, which was backed up in discussion by Tanaka when he visited Asatsu to award it the Frontier account). Germans worked hard and had a tradition of 'musical culture' (hence the agency's choice of the Perspiration series, featuring flamenco, jazz and classical musicians).[10]

That these differences were also reflected in *my* comments as a European on the Agency's creative work shows how much we all rely on this structure of common differences. After all, I pointed out that Germans probably valued their musical tradition more than Americans (in spite of the fact that one of the ads in the Perspiration series featured a black jazz drummer). I had no difficulty in accepting my Japanese colleagues' expectations that Germans would link the Perspiration series with their own (essentialized?) self-image as a hard-working people (making them akin to Japanese themselves). And I could readily see how the straight-to-the-point Home Entertainment series would probably appeal slightly more to an American audience.

The use of these kinds of stereotypes by non-Western peoples to create stylized images of the West has been referred to as 'Occidentalism'.[11] Occidentalism is not just a matter of depicting the Western other in stereotypical static form, however. It involves an ongoing, idealized reformulation by the non-Westerner of his or her own society and culture. This interpretation of the Western other's 'essential' characteristics does not mean, of course, that they are *there* for all to see. Rather, they are constructed as part of an ongoing discourse by the political relations that exist both between and within the societies concerned. It is during this process that fluid, constantly flowing historical contexts are 'converted into a timeless and alien essence.'[12]

Japanese interest in the Western other has had a long history, stemming from the arrival in Japan of the Portuguese in the mid-sixteenth century before being thwarted (and simultaneously fanned) by the more than two-century exclusion policy put into effect by the Tokugawa regime from the early seventeenth to mid-nineteenth centuries. The Meiji Restoration of 1868 led to the start of Japan's modernization and to a fascination with 'things Western' as the Japanese sought first to adopt, then to catch up with, and finally surpass (or so people hoped) Western civilization. In the decade leading up to the Frontier presentation, many businessmen began to feel that they had finally succeeded in their goal. They explained that success in Occidentalist terms, because these could be used to offset the then current trade friction between Japanese and the United States. 'What are you complaining about?' went the logic of the Japanese argument. 'All you have to do is adopt our collective management style, manufacturing standards and business acumen and you, too, can be like us. We got where we are today because we work hard, work together in harmony, and use our intuitive judgement when in a jam.'

The Client Other

It is against this background that the Asatsu account team's interpretation of its proposed ad campaigns should be viewed. Like others working in Japan's advertising industry,[13] the creative team constructed stylized images of the West that were based on their own and fellow account team members' images of themselves as Japanese. At the same time, however, the Orientalisms and Occidentalisms that they created in the different series for the Frontier presentation were shaped by political contingencies. This is where we need to take account of that other 'other' – Asatsu's Japanese client. Throughout its preparations for the presentation, the account team did its best *not* to make a selection from its six main campaign series (until ordered to do so by Tanaka). In a way those concerned wanted to *avoid* making a distinction between two audiences – one in Germany and the other in the United States – which were, according to the normal Japanese ways of thinking outlined above, not clearly distinguished but lumped together as 'Western'. At the same time, though, because it was trying to win its client's account, agency staff needed to find out precisely how those in Frontier themselves defined 'the West', and what images *they* would use to differentiate between Americans and Germans. More specifically, members of the account team had to find out who in particular was responsible for the decision to award, or not to award, Asatsu the Frontier account. The final images – the final Orientalisms and Occidentalisms – used by the account team in its presentation, therefore, depended in large part on the *individual* interpretations of what constituted 'German' and 'American' by two members of Frontier's senior management (Tanaka and Oba).[14]

As a result of these contingencies, Ueda eventually put forward four main ideas.[15] By then he had a pretty good idea that his team's two main choices – the Perspiration (musicians) and Home Entertainment (entertainers outlined against laser and compact discs) series – were approved of by Tanaka, if not Oba. But each of these series also reflected other aspects of the Japanese discourse of the Western other. The Perspiration series was proposed for 'depth' in the Agency's communication strategy because Europe is seen by the Japanese as a repository of 'high culture', and thus of cultural 'depth'. Similarly, the sheer geographical expanse of the United States was reflected in the account team's choice of the Home Entertainment series for 'scope' (*hirogari*), which was also epitomized by the supporting Nature series that made use of visuals of vast expanses of uninhabited American desert.

At the same time, having discarded the Frontier managing director's idea of 'light' (*hikari*) in both its choice of tag line and campaign ideas, Ueda *had* to find something that he knew would appeal to the client's decision-makers. Thus, against the advice of its resident European anthropologist and American copy-writer, he included the Nature series because he knew that it would appeal to both major decision-makers in Frontier (Oba and Tanaka). Why the appeal? Because a number of Japanese writers have suggested that their collective orientation and social structure have emerged from a particular way of life focused on wet rice agriculture, and because of a long Japanese artistic tradition which has focused on nature as a valued element in aesthetic style. Thus the Nature series proposed by Ueda invoked an essential Japanese Orientalism of 'naturalness' that not only posits a trinity of nature, harmony and race, but sets these against 'the West' in numerous different ways, relating to individual-collective, rational-spiritual and nature-technology divides.[16]

In other words, in trying to isolate and express corporate and commodity dif-ferences, the Asatsu account team tried to narrow its client's gaze to *particular kinds* of difference. In this respect, perhaps, we can compare advertising cam-paigns to beauty pageants of all things. They both:

> Organise and focus debate, and in the process of foregrounding particular kinds of dif-ference, they submerge and obscure others by pushing them into the background. They standardise a vocabulary for describing difference, and provide a syntax for its expres-sion, to produce a common frame of organised distinction, in the process making wildly disparate groups of people intelligible to each other. They essentialise some kinds of differences as ethnic, physical and immutable, and portray them as measurable and scalable characteristics, washing them with the legitimacy of objectivity. And they use these distinctions to draw systemic connections between disparate parts of the world system.[17]

What this discussion shows us, I think, is just how difficult it is to separate the ele-ments that go into our own and others' constructions of others (and ourselves). As Lise Skov and I have argued more generally elsewhere,[18] the fact that Asatsu was undertaking a global campaign strategy on behalf of its client merely complicated the way in which the agency's strategic propositions were engaged in a form of essentialist cultural reproduction. Campaigns addressed at American and German target audiences had little choice but to adopt a lingua franca of consumerism which acted as a visual shorthand for specific places, dramas and meanings. In spite of the structure of common differences expected of all advertising cam-paigns, therefore, Orientalist and Occidentalist images end up becoming focal points in a *global stylistic continuity* and tend thus to be the same, whether they are produced in Japan, Europe or the United States.[19] They both integrate the other and are integrated in the other.

The Japanese Other

In spite of this, when Tanaka, the manager from Frontier, came to announce officially that his company had decided to appoint Asatsu as its agency for the international account, one of the things he mentioned towards the end of the meeting was that Asatsu's mode of presentation was 'very Japanese'.

> When you presented your creative strategy and the market analysis you based it on, Ueda, you never ever put your foot down and said you were convinced you were 'right'. That surprised us a bit. After all, we're hardly the experts when it comes to creative work. In this respect, you people at Asatsu were really different from J&M. They fielded three or four foreigners, and when we challenged them on some of the ways they'd interpreted the market, they really stuck to their guns and insisted they were right. I don't know. I just feel I'd like to hear someone in Asatsu insisting that what you're advising a client is absolutely right.

The head of the International Division nodded his head in agreement when he heard this and said with a troubled frown:

> The trouble with advertising is that there's no justification really for anyone to say '*this* is the only way to do things.' J&M might have said so, but my own experience tells me that just isn't the case. So, as a result, you end up with little alternative but to say 'well, this is about right.'

The head of the International Division's response was rather typical of the then prevailing attitude among Asatsu's senior management towards 'foreign influences'. Indeed, when I first met Masao Inagaki and asked if I might study Asatsu, he had mused that the agency needed someone who could 'explain us Japanese to the Americans' (who at the time were engaged in tense negotiations over 'trade friction' between the two countries). But not everyone necessarily believed that 'being Japanese' was the best way to carry out one's work in the advertising world. Three or four junior account executives remarked during the course of my fieldwork that they wished people would be more forthright and say what they meant, instead of evading issues and covering up difficulties with placatory platitudes and flattery. This suggested that, in time, a younger generation of employees would begin to challenge the very 'Japaneseness' on which Asatsu's reputation had been built.

But the 'Japanese' way of doing business was not necessarily bad; nor was it criticized on all counts. The issue of 'Japanese' versus 'Western' ways of doing things came up fairly frequently in other contexts, as you will no doubt recall from an earlier chapter in which stories about client presentations were told. For example, one senior manager commented on Asatsu's winning the PKW account as follows:

> When we were awarded a lucrative and prestigious account by a European client, do you know the first thing we were told to do? We had to set up a separate room over in the Victor Building to house the whole account team. The client insisted on this. It wasn't going to have its advertising campaign handled in the same building as the account of a rival firm. Indeed, the client even tried to get Inagaki to drop the competing Japanese account, even though Asatsu had been handling it for well over a decade. How about that for arrogance?

This story was part of an ongoing discourse (what I earlier called *Tales of reproduction*) among all employees in the Account Services Division, but particularly in its international branch, about how foreigners totally failed to understand or trust Japanese business methods. But it emerged again in the Presidential Office when the CEO and his senior adviser were talking to me one afternoon about the agency's American partner:

> The trouble is our partner seems to have no understanding at all of the principle of mutual stock holding that goes on here in Japan. I mean, when you enter into partnership with another Japanese company, you buy up shares in each other's firms to show goodwill and that you're in it for the long duration. But now our partner says it's going to sell off its Asatsu shares because they're valued high and it wants to make a quick profit. That's not the way we do things, but our partner's CEO doesn't seem to get it. Here at Asatsu, on the other hand, we're going to hold on to our partner's shares for as long as the partnership between us lasts. It's a matter of principle. That's how we do things here in Japan.

And then, one day, Yano himself recounted a story after putting down the telephone in some perplexity after what had clearly been a confusing conversation.

> As you know, *sensei*, I'm the kind of manager who generally prefers a 'Japanese' style of doing business. By which I mean I believe in pursuing business opportunities by means of networking, by making connections and massaging them as opportunity or need arises. And I build up personal relationships based on mutual trust and an acceptance of the principle of what we like to call 'give-and-take' in Japanese-style English.
>
> And that's what you'd expect, isn't it, of other Japanese businessmen working here in Tokyo? But do you know what? I've recently found myself dealing with a Japanese executive who's spent a large part of his working life in the United States. As a result, he's learned to value 'Western-style rationality' over 'Japanese-style emotion' – what, in Japanese, we like to call 'dry' rather than 'wet' personal business relations …

In Japanese business, it's quite normal for one company to invite another company out for a few drinks, or a meal, or even a weekend at a country club. We're all so busy during the daytime and weekdays that we think it appropriate to try to relax a bit over some good food, a few glasses of beer or whisky, or a round or two of golf. After all, business is driven by personal relations and these sorts of leisure activities allow us to get to know one another as *people* and not just as members of this or that company. Do you follow me?

Well, last Saturday, I invited the new advertising manager of a client of ours for a weekend at a country club of which our agency's a member. It was beautiful weather, as you know, and we played a lot of golf, but I'm so bad he won all the time. You know how it is in Japan, *sensei*. When you play golf, you use the occasion to talk about business. Which is exactly what I did. At one stage yesterday morning, therefore, when we were out on the course, I broached the idea of a new advertising campaign to my companion who seemed very pleased with the idea and appeared to give me the go-ahead. But this morning, when I mentioned our deal on the phone just now, the manager asked me: 'What deal?' And when I reminded him of what we'd talked about on the golf course, he curtly replied: 'That was on the golf course. Business deals are made in the office, not on the golf course.' Can you believe it?

At the heart of stories like these lay an ongoing discourse about what Japanese ad men liked to call 'sleeping skills' (*newaza* in Japanese):

Advertising accounts here in Japan are all about 'sleeping skills'. 'Human chemistry' is how I like to translate it into English when I have to explain to foreigners how we do things here in Japan. That's what interpersonal relations are all about. It's human chemistry that underpins long-term relations, consistency, 'humanity' and all those other things we value in Japanese firms.

And 'sleeping skills' stand in stark contract to the kind of 'stand up skills' (*tachiwaza*) or 'professionalism' you find in American and other Western business relations. I mean, that isn't to say that Americans don't make use of human chemistry. Of course they do. And it doesn't mean, either, that we Japanese aren't professional in our dealings with clients. It's just that each of us places different emphases on them both.

I suppose, in the long run, you could say that Japanese business is two thirds chemistry and one third professionalism. With Americans, it's the other way round: two thirds professionalism and one third human chemistry. But the gap's narrowing – mainly because so many Japanese companies are sending their staff abroad. And then it's a matter of when in Rome (*gō ni ireba*) …

The kind of ongoing stories related here clearly engaged with how the Japanese advertising industry was in important ways *perceived* to be (although not necessarily *was* in practice) rather different from advertising industries found elsewhere in the world. They also for the most part sustained Asatsu's distinctive reputation for being a very 'Japanese' agency (a point made to me by the advertising sales manager of the Hokkaido Newspaper who first suggested that I study there and who then introduced me to Inagaki).[20] Finally, they also hinted at a more general discourse that was just then emerging among Japanese businessmen (and remember, all this took place just as the Japanese economy was entering a sustained period of recession that lasted through the 1990s into the new millennium) about whether in fact their 'Japanese' model of doing business – a model that had been at the very heart of Japan's remarkable post-war economic growth – was superior to, or should in some respects be supplanted by, the Anglo-American 'free market' economic model.[21]

An Authentic Conclusion?

At the heart of these different takes on 'the other' that I have presented in this chapter is the issue of *authenticity*, which itself takes us back to my discussion of how an advertising agency (and indeed almost all other business organizations) is very concerned with how best to manage impressions. This it needs to do on two fronts. The first, as we have seen, is in its social interaction with a client. Here, as we have noted time and time again, impression management has virtually nothing to do with the consumers at which a client's advertising campaign is to be directed, and everything to do with the client company itself, and its representatives. An agency has to convince its prospective client that it is genuinely trying to understand the client's marketing problem and that the steps it is taking to address that problem in a series of advertising campaigns displays the agency's overall expertise and professionalism.

Thus, during preparations for the Frontier presentation, I was co-opted as a 'real' Westerner to help conceptualize an 'elusive, inadequately defined, other cultural, socially ordered genuineness'[22] that the account team believed it needed to persuade Frontier to award Asatsu its prestigious account. The account team's creative ideas were thus authenticated by my own 'Western' presence. It did not matter in the end what I (or the American copywriter) thought of the various visual ideas. The account team chose what it calculated Frontier's decision-makers would like best. But the fact that I was a visible member of the account team would make it seem to the client that the agency's choice was indeed an authentic reflection of 'the West', precisely because I was a Westerner. The measure of authenticity here was the person used and judged in these power relations.[23]

The way in which the Asatsu account team interacted with its future client, Frontier, in the construction of both advertising images and agency professionalism parallels the type of 'authenticity work' and need for professionalism in the career of a Spanish film director, Pedro Almodóvar, as described by Silviya Svejenova.[24] It also supports another argument that, because so little is known about what judgemental criteria are used by decision-makers to assess the creative potential of pitches (by Hollywood scriptwriters), and because the interpersonal nature of the pitching process is clearly important in the final assessment of 'creativity', those making a pitch need to strategically tailor their behaviour in order to activate audience participation and engagement, if they are to get their work accepted.[25]

But an ad agency also needs to manage impressions on a second front: that of advertising itself. After all, its job is to make a particular piece of stereo equipment, beer or perfume stand out in such a way that we consumers are persuaded to buy it the next time we visit a store. In this respect, an agency is a key maker of meanings linking producers with consumers. And yet most of the evidence provided in this book suggests that advertising personnel are not *that* interested in consumers, unless a purported understanding of them will help them in the more important task of persuading a potential client to part with its money. If there is any fetishization, then, it is of the client, rather than of the consumer.

That advertising images should eventually seem to manage consumers' impressions, however, has led to considerable criticism on the part of academics. Over several decades, one scholar after another has argued that the increased use of images in advertising 'blurs rather than sharpens the outlines of reality', leading to what Daniel Boorstin called 'the appeal of the contrived'.[26] Advertising appropriates people's 'real' experiences, needs and desires and gives them 'false' content, by systematically associating 'pure' cultural symbols with 'the profane world of commerce'.[27] As a result, advertising imagery is never of actual, but only of idealized, human beings.[28] Even when constructing 'authenticity' as a powerful sign in our everyday commodity culture (Coke as 'the real thing'), advertising 'devalues' our individual experiences because, on the one hand, they are made to seem reproducible in all other consumers,[29] and because, on the other, the fluidity of commodity culture turns today's 'authenticity' into tomorrow's 'falseness'.[30] By using 'believability' to displace 'truth',[31] advertising images are seen to constitute us as one of the objects that, as consumers, we ourselves then have to exchange. In this process, 'advertisements alienate our identity'.[32] Ultimately, advertising signs indicate the absence of both human relationships and real objects.[33]

What the Frontier case study shows is that, as often as not, it is *people* and not *products* that drive the production and selection of images in commodity culture. Moreover, it is *the producer* – that is to say, the client as financial sponsor – rather than *the consumer* who is being addressed by advertising images in the first instance. It is the likes and dislikes of key decision-making personnel in a client company that an ad agency has to discover and satisfy if it is to gain the account on offer. It is only success in this particular piece of impression management that *then* enables an agency to address – and possibly alienate – consumers. In other words, the social world of advertising production also needs to be taken into account in discussions of images used in advertising campaigns, for authenticity as such is 'located in neither the creator nor the creative product but rather in the interaction between the creator and the field's gatekeepers who selectively retain or reject original products.'[34] It is the systems of production, representation, distribution *and* consumption that together shape both authenticity and creativity in advertising and other fields of symbolic production.[35]

–7–

Ethnography at Work

This book – like the advertising practices it describes – has been an exercise not just in 'thick description', as Clifford Geertz so famously put it, but also in thick interpretation.[1] Having presented you with what I called a 'case study' detailing how a Japanese advertising agency's account team went about preparing for a competitive presentation to a major Japanese electronics corporation, I then proceeded to go off on a number of different theoretical tangents. These covered several seemingly disparate, but ultimately inter-connected, phenomena:

1. The social effects, both within an agency and between agency, client and media organization, arising from how money is distributed in the advertising industry by means of accounts.

2. The ways in which advertising people tell stories about accounts, about their agency and about the industry in which they work as a way of structuring the fleeting moments of their everyday lives.

3. Many of these stories centre on competitive presentations in which agency employees are, or have been, involved. These presentations are regularly held dramaturgical performances in the advertising industry when those participating seek to manage the impressions they give off to would-be and existing clients in order to gain the latter's trust and business.

4. As part of their preparations for a presentation, an account team – which consists of 'humdrum' account executives, market analysts and media buyers, on the one hand and, on the other, of 'creative' copywriters and art directors – needs to prepare mock advertising campaigns. The creative ideas that form these advertisements tend to be constrained by a number of fixed material, temporal, physical, social, ideological and economic conditions.

5. These conditions include the almost inherent tension between account and creative personnel, on the one hand, and those between agency and client, on the other. Thus the contents of any one advertising campaign, or even single advertisement, tend not to be directed at the consumer in the first instance. Instead, advertising personnel need to be able to gauge accurately the various different 'others' with whom they come into contact during the course of preparations for an ad campaign. These 'others' may be a fellow member of the account team, or

115

senior manager within the agency concerned, but are more likely targeted decision-making executives in the client company. They are also, finally, targeted consumers who, in the case of the Frontier presentation, were non-Japanese and who therefore presented a problem of Orientalist and Occidentalist interpretations of proposed campaign ideas.

Such interpretations are not limited to those working in the advertising industry, but affect anyone – like myself – trying to understand those interpretations. This raises an issue of representation. How does one go about describing the things people do during their everyday lives? And how does the way in which I choose to describe the case study presented here vary from other possible ways of presenting the same material? In this final chapter, I want to try to round things off by looking briefly at the role of ethnography in research, and at how ethnography may be a useful tool for business people trying to understand, analyse and strategically plan for the world in which they work.

As you may recall, at the very end of my description of Asatsu's preparations for its presentation to Frontier, I posed a number of questions that I promised to try to answer in the ensuing chapters. The final paragraph of Chapter 1 read as follows:

> This case study hinges on my own participation in on-going events and the contribution that I was able to make, with a little help from my friends, to Asatsu's successful presentation to Frontier. This raises a methodological issue. What is the role of the participant observer in anthropological fieldwork? How much should s/he observe? How much should s/he participate? And how is one to blend the two? Are there any advantages to this kind of research in business organizations that other researchers might learn from? Isn't ethnographic fieldwork something that anyone going into business should practise as a matter of course in his or her everyday working life? Isn't a successful manager no less than a practising – and practised – fieldworker?

Characteristics of Fieldwork

Let me start with fieldwork. What does it consist of? How does one go about it? And what are its dis/advantages vis-à-vis other methods of doing research?[2]

Anthropologists have recognized fieldwork as a viable research methodology for many decades now, and generally uphold it as a (at one stage, before scholars from neighbouring disciplines like sociology and cultural studies also practised it, *the*) distinguishing feature of their discipline. Although occasionally – and, I think in the long run, justifiably – accused of fetishizing fieldwork as a research method, anthropologists generally regard it as being marked by four exceptional characteristics:

1. As its defining feature, perhaps, fieldwork demands *intensive participant observation*.[3]
2. Fieldwork cannot be conducted by means of long-distance communication, but requires that the researcher be physically present – what Clifford Geertz has referred to as 'being there' – and undergo *total* (or near total) *social immersion*.[4]
3. The *duration* of that physical presence is also critical; it should be long-term – ideally about a year.[5]
4. The combination of the above three characteristics gives rise, ideally, to an *intimacy* between researcher and informants not provided by other research methods.[6] This intimacy tends to lead to the acquisition of high-quality data that cannot be replicated by any other research method.

The four features of intensive participant observation, total social immersion, long-term duration and informant intimacy are ideals that are practised to a greater or lesser extent depending on the particular circumstances in which each fieldworker finds herself. In my own case, for example, I have generally been quite fortunate and found that the intensive participant observation bit has worked rather well. When studying the ceramic art market, I was able to hold my own pottery exhibition in a department store and so experienced first hand many of the paradoxes arising from the 'unholy alliance' of money and art that I had heard about from potter informants.[7] By being able to come up with what was generally accepted as a rather apt tag line and one or two other ideas for Asatsu's Frontier presentation, too, I found myself invited by other account executives in the agency to take part in and contribute to a number of other ongoing projects, ranging from dreaming up a name and associated services for All Nippon Airways' business class (*Club ANA*) to devising a marketing and creative concept for a Nihon Lever fabric softener (*Happiness is a Soft Blanket*).

This ability on my part to make a contribution to informants' everyday problems encouraged a number of people to treat me thenceforth more as an ad man than as just a university professor in the way that they had done until then. As a result, I was able to begin to put together the numerous pieces of information that I had gathered during the Frontier presentation preparations and fit them into various theoretical jigsaw puzzles of the kind you have been reading about in this book. In a way, then, the Frontier case marked a subtle shift in my role as fieldwork researcher. Instead of being a participant observer in the classic anthropological manner, I became an observant participant. Although not too much is said about this sort of thing in anthropological literature, observant participation should, I believe, be the ideal to which we all aspire during our research.

Now, it may seem to one or two of my readers that there isn't that much of a distinction to be made between participant observation and observant participation, and that I am merely splitting hairs by stressing the importance of the latter. But what I want to get across is the fact that this distinction – however crude or subtle it may seem – in fact marks an important *rite de passage* in fieldwork itself and affects the *quality* of information given and later analysed. *The* problem facing any researcher – whether she be anthropologist, sociologist, historian, political scientist, or whatever – is the validity of materials gathered. Does this survey ask the right kind of questions so far as the research hypothesis is concerned? Is this historical document dug up in a castle attic as authentic as it seems, or is it a fake – written deliberately with a quill pen on parchment to pull the wool over an unsuspecting reader's eyes? Is this informant telling me what he really does in a particular situation, or what he should be doing, but in fact does not do? In every field of study scholars have to wrestle with such problems of validity.

In fieldwork, the real difficulty facing the anthropologist is trying to distinguish between what people *say* they do and what they actually *do*. Indeed, this is the problem facing all those in management and organization studies who make use of interviews as a primary research material. As we saw in Chapter 4, people are always trying to manage impressions and to put across an image that may in fact be rather different from that of their 'real' selves. This is fairly easy to do when their interviewer has just walked in off the street with a series of prepared questions to ask during the next hour. It becomes less so when that same interviewer had been hanging around the office for the past three months, watching what is going on and asking questions of anyone who has the time or inclination to talk to her. For her own part, the fieldworker is desperately trying to make sense of this new social world into which, for one reason or another, she has made her way. What those around her take for granted as 'the normal course of events' often strikes her as not just strange, but from another planet. In a slightly different sense from that originally intended by Oliver Sacks, the fieldworker may well feel as if she's an 'anthropologist on Mars'.

What marks the shift from participant observation to observant participation, I think, is precisely the ability to see beyond the social front that informants present to strangers in their everyday lives, to know that there is a difference between 'front-stage' and 'back-stage' behaviour, and to have ready access to that back stage. Moreover, your informants realize that you know and, as a result, stop pretending when in your presence and allow themselves to be seen as they are. This is immensely helpful to the fieldworker in terms of the quality of research she is able to conduct, and therefore of the quality of analysis that follows. Thus, in my own case, once I had done my bit in the Frontier presentation and came to be seen as an ad man, I was – so to speak – accepted by agency employees as 'one of them', rather than as an outsider. This led to my being given free access to informal, inside knowledge of agency-client and agency-media relations, as well as of Asatsu's own organizational features. Although, of course, there is no guarantee that length of fieldwork in itself will bring about the passage from participant observation to observant participation, this shift from front stage to back stage would never have been possible without the long-term duration of my fieldwork.[8]

In spite of these 'successes', however, total social immersion and intimacy have depended very much on the type of fieldwork being conducted.[9] For example, in a rural community in southern Japan where I lived with my family for four years, our lives were entirely sucked up by community affairs. During these goings-on, all of us developed close friendships with local potters, farmers, foresters and their wives and children and shared in their daily mis/fortunes.[10] In the advertising agency, however, the situation was rather different. For a start, there is a limit to the amount of time anyone in any walk of life – even the most devoted banker, shop owner or academic – spends in his place of work. Even though, from time to time, I would stay late at my desk on weekday evenings, and occasionally go into Asatsu on a Saturday to see who else was there, doing what with whom, while overtly catching up on my notes, I rarely put in the long hours of overtime that were customary for my informants. Nor did I ever meet them in their home environment. The nearest thing I got to an invitation to *extramural* activities was the rare quick drink in a neighbourhood bar and occasional slap-up meal with Yano who took me along as an 'interesting rarity' to help entertain a client.

If my fieldwork in Asatsu was not entirely true to the ideal of total social immersion – a feature that has come under some scrutiny in recent years[11] – it was marked by the development of quite close working relationships with individual personnel in the agency. It is almost certainly the quality of such relationships that influences what kind of findings and insights a fieldworker gets, and I will leave you to judge that quality in my own case from the material presented in this book. The intimacy developed with 'informants', however, is very important because it helps show people not as one-dimensional research subjects, but as rounded individuals.[12] I suspect that such intimacy (which reveals both positive and negative aspects of a person's character) is easier to come by in frame-based fieldwork, such as that conducted in a remote mountain valley,[13] than in the kind of network-based fieldwork that made up much of my research in Asatsu.

The fact that the people one is studying *do* turn out to be multi-faceted, so that they can talk about a weekend game of football in almost the same breath as plotting how to get a client to come round to a particular creative proposition, has certain reverberations for the researcher when she comes to writing up her analysis of the data that she's collected. Business people often think, and sometimes complain, that anthropologists – indeed, academics in general – are long winded and fail to get to the point. As someone who has had to sit through endless lectures, seminars and meetings of all kinds during the past two and a half decades, I have a lot of sympathy for this point of view. Few academics are succinct; not many are able to express complex ideas in a reasonably audience-friendly manner; and some fail to get to the point because they have no point to make. But many business people also think that it is a waste of their valuable time having to read anything that is more than a one-page summary of a longer report, with bullet points to aid speed reading. This is, to put it mildly, a little short-sighted of them.

Of course, if you *want* to follow television news formats and reduce life to one page bullet points, that is your affair. But if you're a business executive in charge of the working lives of a more or less large number of people, then you have a duty to try to understand those people. And understanding and the resolution of complex issues do not, alas, come from a casual reading of bullet points. Whether you like it or not, whether you are 'too busy' or not, you have to delve further. This, I think, is where the kind of ethnography practised by anthropologists can come in really useful. They have to write up their material in a reasonably readable form, of course, and organize their analyses coherently, but what they have to say is multi-faceted, complex, nuanced and revealing. It also shows just how difficult it is to separate 'right' from 'wrong', which is total anathema to business managers charged with making the 'quick decision'. But more of that in a while.

Fieldwork and Case Studies

As you will by now realize, fieldwork tends to be a 'messy, qualitative experience'[14] – a far cry from the kind of (pseudo-?) scientific research methods taught in business schools and published in numerous long-selling textbooks around the world. I doubt if many anthropologists, for example, rigorously follow the nine steps of observation and literature review; problem clarification; assumptions and hypotheses; concept, constructs and models; research design; data collection; data analysis; interpretations and conclusions; and improvement in theory of problem solving outlined by Pervez Ghauri and Kjell Grønhaug as part of 'the wheel of research'.[15] But this doesn't mean that they do not 'read around' and come up with one or two hypotheses prior to going to the field to collect data, which they then analyse and interpret with conclusions. However, they do tend to be wary of 'concepts, constructs and models' and probably don't get too worried about 'improvement in theory or problem solving', if only because the qualitative, messy and ad hoc nature of fieldwork reveals the former as artificial constructs that bear little relation to reality and the latter as unattainable ideals, given the different individual project orientations of the methodology adopted.

Not all research methods recommended in business studies literature, however, are so scientific. The case study method, for example, is made to balance acrobatically on the high wire dividing scientific surveys and questionnaires from more or less chaotic fieldwork. Its adoption is based on the principle that different research strategies need different methods of research. Much depends on:

1. The type of research questions.
2. Control of the researcher over behavioural events.
3. Focus of the research on contemporary, as opposed to historical, issues.
4. The kind of information sought.
5. How this information can best be obtained.[16]

When the kind of research question posed is 'who, what, where, how many, how much?' then a survey is probably most appropriate. If, on the other hand, the answer to the question 'how?' or 'why?' is sought, then you can either use an experiment (when you want to control behavioural events), or a case study (when you don't). A case study is also to be preferred when the focus of your research is on a contemporary issue in a real life context. In the end, defining the research questions is seen as the most important step of all.[17]

In spite of the fact that case studies are often dismissed for being 'merely' exploratory, descriptive or explanatory (remember those students of mine way back at the beginning of this book),[18] they probably should be adopted to resolve most of the problems affecting managers and the companies in which they work. Why do ordinary employees take so little interest in their work or in helping one another out, and how can this be changed? How can we improve our monthly sales figures? Why did we get in the mess we're in? What kinds of people make the best managers for our company, and how can we find them? These are the sorts of questions to which no questionnaire, survey, experiment, archival research or 'in-depth' interview is going to be able to give a satisfactory answer. Each may produce pat answers, maybe, but not ones that will prove useful in the long term by helping us deal with the problem to hand.

The when-to-use-a-case-study approach makes good sense. After all, my own ethnographic study of Asatsu came about because of one very simple question, hitherto not properly posed or answered in the literature I had read: How is an advertisement actually made? This led to further questions, like: Why are particular images, headlines, slogans and tag lines adopted, and not others? Who is responsible for selection of the final images? What are the overall social processes that lie behind the advertising campaigns that we see on television, glance at in our newspapers or magazines, or hear on the radio?

The assumption that I then made, based on common sense, was that the answer to these questions lay in an advertising agency. By doing fieldwork in an advertising agency, I reasoned, I would find myself in a pivotal organization within the advertising industry as a whole, and therefore be able to learn all about the latter, too. At the same time, my questions constructed the field of research that I was to enter. I would be based in an advertising agency, but forage for further research fodder among radio and television stations, newspaper and magazine publishers, client offices, studios of one sort or another, model agencies, and so on. Together these constituted my fieldwork in – and the field of – Japanese advertising.

Case studies are also criticized for providing little basis for scientific generalizations.[19] This, I think, depends very much on the quality of the data obtained and the kind of analysis conducted. As we have seen in the chapters of this book, sound analysis of rich case material can lead to all kinds of generalizations, and even one or two predictions. For example, the amount of leeway given a creative team is likely to depend on prevailing economic conditions and the kind of account system prevailing in the country concerned. This will necessarily affect the creativity of an ad campaign. When the national economy is good, clients are prepared to spend money on advertising and permit their agencies to experiment with ideas; when there is a recession and money is tight, agencies are held on a tight leash. Where a competing account system prevails, an agency is always more likely to be free of client control than in a country like Japan where the norm is for a client to split its advertising account among competing agencies.

Is there a difference, then, between a case study and fieldwork? It seems that there is and there isn't, depending on which particular scholar favours which point of view. So far as I myself am concerned, case studies are particular forms of research that can occur from time to time during a longer period of all-encompassing fieldwork. They focus on particular events – preparations for an ad campaign, a competitive presentation, an art exhibition, a studio shoot – which are often dramaturgical in the context of the field being studied, and whose particularities can be used to make generalizations about the field as a whole. In other words, a case study is a 'social situation' because it can be analysed in its relation to other social situations,[20] and so enable the researcher to build up a total overall picture of a particular field of study.

This is what I have tried to do in this book. By starting with an account team's preparations for a competitive presentation, I have been able to move to a discussion of the social consequences of the financial structure of the advertising industry as a whole, before analysing how both industry and organization structure of the agency is sustained – and occasionally questioned – by means of different kinds of stories. I then showed how people working in an advertising agency are very concerned – as are those in business organizations in general – to make not just an impression, but the right kind of impression, on those with whom they are doing business. This often means second-guessing the likes and dislikes of both clients and – in this case, foreign – consumers, whom copywriters and art directors strive to please with work that they try to make out as being more 'creative' than it actually is, given the conditions under which they work. Having started, then, with a small group of agency employees, I ended up discussing and analysing not just the advertising industry as a whole, but how Japanese go about imagining the West. Have I been overly ambitious?

Very little of this would have been possible if I had not already spent a dozen or so years living in Japan (and if I hadn't been fluent in the spoken and written language, of course). If, for example, I had wanted to study preparations for an ad campaign and had then waited until an opportune moment presented itself, I doubt whether I'd have got very far. I needed to have experienced already a little of how the ad industry works in Japan – and by experience I mean physical experience, not a mental dabbling in written words – or the preparations wouldn't have made *that* much sense to me. In other words, I was helped immensely by watching what people did and how they did it, as well as by the stories circulating around my desk and recounted in Chapter 3, together with one or two off-the-cuff remarks about front stage and backstage behaviour (which is a commonly made distinction in everyday Japanese relations). All this helped orientate me when I was allowed to join the Frontier presentation account team. So far as I myself am concerned, therefore, case studies are most successful when they form part of more general fieldwork. Without that fieldwork, you may not be lost exactly, but you're likely to stray when it comes to a case.

I guess this is the real difference between my own anthropological approach and what advertisers and marketers now call 'ethnography'. Marketing analysts make use of case studies as they delve into particular issues and use their results to persuade clients to do one thing or another. One worldwide advertising agency, for example, once asked me to conduct a series of extended interviews to find out about men's grooming habits in Japan. These interviews were based on a range of pre-defined questions that were simultaneously administered to similar groups of men in two other countries (the study was intended to be comparative). In addition, informants were asked to show me various parts of the apartments or houses in which they lived, to talk about the products they used, and then to visit a local store to comment on what they saw on display there, as well as to buy a few items themselves. The whole meeting was filmed on video camera, dubbed into English and prepared for playback to agency personnel and client who could then judge for themselves from what they saw and heard.

Although initially a bit sceptical of this 'in-depth-interview-plus-a-bit-of-field-work' approach, I was ultimately quite impressed with the data obtained and the analysis that emerged (I guess I had to be impressed since the latter in particular was my own work!). This was mainly because I was able, as an anthropologist, to make use of my broad-based knowledge of things Japanese to interpret and analyse what my informants told or showed me. In this respect, therefore, an ethnographic case study of the kind currently hyped by marketers can be extremely productive, although we have to accept that there is no way of knowing for sure whether interviewees are being entirely up-front in what they say. Ethnography also needs prior expertise on the part of the researcher, I think, to make it work effectively. And by 'expertise', I mean a training in analysing interpersonal and institutional relations, together with a broader understanding of the society and culture in which they are embedded.

Managers as Fieldworkers

In the end, hardly any of what I have written in the previous paragraphs should strike my patient businessman readers as particularly novel. Hopefully most of my reflections will have fallen under the rubric of 'common sense'. I say this because I believe that fieldwork or 'ethnography' is not peculiar to particular disciplines in the academic profession, but is something actively practised in the world of business. I'm sorry, fellow anthropologists, but that's the way it is!

Generally speaking, one can draw parallels between research and managerial problem solving. Both need first to decide what it is they wish to achieve, before collecting relevant facts and information to help them reach this objective. They then have to analyse the data they've gathered, decide what's relevant and what not, and proceed to structure their analysis in such a way that they achieve their goal and/or initiate different action. In the words of a couple of European business school professors: 'This process, deciding what to do, collecting information, discarding irrelevant information, analysing the relevant information and arriving at a conclusion/decision in a systematic procedure, is useful for the cumulative knowledge as well as of the personal development of the researcher and manager alike.'[21]

So far, so good. But I think we can go much further in this comparison by saying that managers are in fact practising fieldworkers. Because they are working for an organization of one sort or another, and are charged with the management of a particular sphere of that organization's daily operations, managers *participate* intensively in the daily lives of those with whom s/he works. At the same time, precisely because they are charged with managerial duties, they are required to *observe* what is going on around them. In this respect, they fulfil the first requirement of fieldwork: that of intensive participant observation. Moreover, because they are so actively involved in what is going on and because they move easily between front stage and back stage, managers are very much observant participants. That is their job. Otherwise, they couldn't possibly be effective managers.

But managers also quickly fulfil the other three sine qua nons of fieldwork outlined earlier: total immersion, long-term duration, and intimacy with informants. They work the basic hours of nine to five, or whatever the norm in their particular organization is, and usually add on a few extra hours (again following norms). They do so day in, day out, with customary breaks for weekends, over many years (unless they are inveterate job hoppers) and so get to know their fellow workers fairly well – their personal strengths and weaknesses, likes and dislikes, and so on. Of course, their immersion is not *total* because managers, like most normal people, have families, hobbies and interests that give them 'a break' from work. But still, for those ambitious ones who want to 'get somewhere' in their lives, immersion in work is seen to be very important. And, as they spend their time in the office, whether they are workaholics or adopt a more relaxed approach to their job, like ethnographers, they laboriously construct the field of which they are a part – working out organizational relationships, individuals' hidden motives affecting particular courses of action, and the strategic advantages to be gained from this kind of decision or that bit of impression management.

The managerial experience, then, like the ethnographic experience, is open-ended. In a way, therefore, their education – like the anthropologist's – is based on a series of case studies. Things are fundamentally ad hoc – part deliberate, part laissez-faire, part negotiated, part left to chance – with the occasional step back to 'take stock'. However much a manager might like it, s/he has no firm control over what goes on. Like the academic ethnographer, therefore, s/he needs to adopt a nuanced, shifting, multiple-sided personality that is able to 'respond and adapt flexibly to social situations as they arise, to be open to a wide variety of different types of relationships and interaction.'[22] Every manager, too, experiences the tension between personal and professional aspects of his work – as Yano's description of his failed business negotiations on the golf course clearly showed.

The way in which managers deal with personnel under their supervision, too, resembles the researcher-informant relationship in several important ways. After all, they always need to provide as complete a picture as possible of the work they're involved in to enable those concerned to participate fully. They need to communicate effectively in simple language, to provide room for questions and be prepared to listen, because what is at stake is the building of a relationship of trust between manager and other employees. This means making sure that anonymity and confidentiality are assured as appropriate, and that one is always as objective as possible in a situation. Deception or coercion will get a manager nowhere in the long term.[23]

Ethics, then, are a common issue in the work of both managers and ethnographers. We owe it to those we study or have authority over to be honest in our endeavours, accurate in our analyses. We shouldn't pretend that things are what they're not, or aren't what they are. Nor should we suggest that things are clear-cut when they aren't (or we don't think they are). It probably helps to make sure others know our weaknesses (if we're aware of them ourselves, that is). These are ideals, of course. One problem, as we saw in the Frontier case study, is that managers are often caught up in organizational politics of one kind or another. One set of ideals can thus become distorted as different ideals take over to fit individual purposes. Take this book, for example. You may legitimately ask: Why did Moeran choose to write *this* kind of book? Was it out of a disinterested desire to make 'pure knowledge' available, and to persuade people that ethnography really is a useful, practical tool in our everyday lives? Or was it more to do with internal politics and a felt need to impress his seemingly more business-oriented colleagues in a European business school? Why focus in this chapter on *managers*? Has he got nothing to say that will be of interest to his professional anthropology colleagues? Isn't he adopting the typical business school academic stance of toadying up to those who might then call on his services and pay him a fat consultancy fee? And so on.

In spite of the fact that managers are, ideally, adroit fieldworkers, this does not mean that they can do without the professional expertise of trained anthropologists and sociologists (you see, I *am* angling for that consultancy fee!). There *is* a difference, I think, between the two professions, if only because the latter have been trained to spot links between relationships, events, and things that appear at first glance to be unconnected. It is these hidden links that can illuminate otherwise confusing social situations. In this sense, perhaps, researchers are trained observers who can use their observations systematically to present results that can be argued over and challenged. At the same time, these observations often scrutinize and lay bare the non- or only semi-conscious ideals and beliefs of participants that often pass for 'common sense'.[24] And although common sense may be common to most (but by no means all) of those concerned, it is not necessarily as sensible to others as it is to its supporters. So, long-term duration as a characteristic of anthropological fieldwork has its limits. If you stay *too* long, you get sucked into the system, so to speak, and fail to distinguish the wood for the trees. This is why anthropologists go off somewhere (not necessarily somewhere far away) to conduct their research before coming back to roost about a year or so later. They need to put physical and mental *distance* between their social immersion in one initially strange way of life and their social immersion back home. Each makes them reflect on the whys and wherefores of the other, although they tend to write about the alien 'other' and not about home comforts.

The only way managers can mimic anthropologists in this respect is by quitting one job and moving on to another. This allows them to reflect on how things used to be in the place(s) they were before, and to analyse situations a bit more objectively than they would otherwise have been able. If they're particularly sharp, they can make use of these employment moves to their advantage by applying their analyses of past situations to what they currently experience.

As you will have gathered from the chapters in this book, a fieldworker tends to use induction as a means of theorizing his data, for it is the information gathered that leads him to see and explain things in a particular way. Most managers, too, are necessarily inductive in their thinking when theirs is 'hands on' experience, which is why they may clash with 'top-down' decisions based on deduction (i.e. usually on what has happened in other companies in similar situations). The question of whether data precede theory, or theory the observations is an old chestnut. Good managers, like good ethnographers, should be doing both all the time, although one always comes across different types. Some managers, like some scholars, stick to their guns regardless (*tenacity*); others use their position to come to a particular decision (*authority*); yet others rely on what they like to call 'gut feeling' (*intuition*); and an occasional few irritatingly insist on a thorough examination of all known facts to arrive at an 'irrefutable' assessment of what is going on (the so-called *scientific approach*).[25] Get all four types of manager in one room to discuss what to do about a particular issue and Buddha alone knows what the result will be. Fortunately, anthropologists tend to work alone. Their clashes are limited to the occasional conference or seminar paper.

End Word

Enough is enough, although it's hard to tell sometimes when best to call it a day while writing a book. There is a terrible urge for an author to try to say something really 'deep' in a Conclusion, when all s/he has to hand are a few more banalities with which to fill in the reader's day. So I'll limit myself to two points here.

Point one. You will have noted that I have throughout this book stressed *people* and not some vague, ill-defined and all-encompassing notion of (corporate) culture. I really feel quite strongly that it's time we put the bugbear of culture aside and moved on. As everyone in Asatsu – and, indeed, in most Japanese companies – well knows, an organization consists of people and it is what people say and do that matters. They are the ones who need to be helped, encouraged, praised, cajoled, managed and very occasionally told off; the ones with whom you share your ups and downs, your hopes and aspirations, your anxieties and fears, your successes and failures. Through their ability and preparedness to take advantage of situations (as well as of competitors), imagine hitherto unimagined opportunities and manipulate the occasional rule, people make or break organizations. For those interested in finding out how their company works, culture's a red herring – a smart bit of impression management that gets us going in ever-diminishing circles until, like the Wok Wok bird, we disappear up our fundamental wotsits without having discovered *precisely* what the role of corporate culture is, how it can be created and sustained, when and how long it might be of use, why it does or does not function effectively in different situations. The search for this particular holy grail of management theory is as elusive as the fabled treasure that my grandfather swore lay at either end of the rainbows that punctured the skies of Tipperary in my childhood.

Point two. What I've tried to do in this final chapter is demystify the fieldwork experience a little and make ethnography into something that can be readily appreciated by anyone who wants to take up a job, is already employed, or is thinking of starting up her own business. This may well be anathema to many anthropologists, who could as a result feel the supposedly solid ground of their methodology trembling beneath their feet – like the occasional tremor of a distant earthquake here in Japan where I write. How dare advertisers and marketers hijack our precious concept of fieldwork, label it ethnography, and use it for their own unscrupulous ends, I hear them moan. That's not *real* ethnography; just a typical quick fix.

Blah, blah, blah…

Notes

Chapter 1

1. E.g. Barthel (1988); Goffman (1979); Goldman (1993); O'Barr (1994); and Williamson (1978), among others.

2. See Moeran (1996a).

3. For details of how I entered Asatsu and then struck up a friendship with Yano, see Moeran (2005a: 83–94).

4. The fiscal year for many, if not all, Japanese companies begins in January and ends in December. What I call the 'corporate year', however, runs from April (when new employees are recruited) to March.

5. It is by no means unusual for advertising campaigns to address an advertiser's employees as well as its consumer targets. Walmart, for example, has *had* to engage in television advertising in order to communicate effectively with its 1.4 million employees.

6. Or account planners. In Japanese, they are called by the rather more down-to-earth title of 'salesmen'.

7. 'Dummy' copy is often used in presentations since a competing agency is not usually given all the information required for it to write the body copy of an advertisement. In other words, what is usually presented by an agency to its client at a competitive pitch is one or more series of visuals, headlines and slogans.

8. Cf. de Mooij (1998: 272–4).

9. In this respect, the post-mortem meeting differs somewhat from Kunda's account (1992: 101) of the 'post-meeting' in HiTech that marked a shift from presentation ritual to routine work, although both allow participants to draw their own meanings from what has just gone on.

10. As Miller (1997: 96) points out – and I myself have noted in my discussion of a Japanese advertising agency (Moeran 1996a) – it is these 'small worlds' of business contacts that continuously interfere with the logic of profitability.

11. It was abundantly clear that the Agency had an extremely good communication channel, or 'pipe', to someone in Frontier (cf. Moeran 1996a: 87–8).

12. De Saussure (1983: 114).

13. Ibid., pp. 121–5.

14. I later learned that he actually had had the tag line checked in the US.

Chapter 2

1. Schudson (1984: 47); Clark (1988: 51).

2. Jones (1999: 9).

3. Cf. Tellis (1998: 66–7).

4. Clark (1988: 47); Jackall and Hirota (2000: 117).

5. Mayle (1990: 13).

6. Cf. Moeran (2005a: 83–131).

7. Jackall and Hirota (2000: 95).

8. This kind of approach, therefore, avoids the purely cultural explanations that have so often been used to explain Japanese advertising (e.g. Mosdell 1986; O'Barr 1994: 157–98).

9. In Europe and the United States, a few very large corporations such as Procter and Gamble divide their products into different lines or brands, each of which is assigned to a different advertising agency (along the general lines of the Japanese split-account system). This enables them to compare the performance of the agencies concerned and to exert on them the kind of power discussed below for Japanese advertisers and their agencies. At the same time, it can be argued that, as far as advertising is concerned, each product line constitutes a separate unit that may be seen as a separate account (Hower 1939: 356).

10. Michell (1988: 15–16).

11. Hower (1939: 354).

12. Foreign advertisers, however, are so concerned – much to the consternation of Japanese agencies when asked to handle their accounts in Japan.

13. A method also known to N.W. Ayer & Son in the second quarter of this century (cf. Hower 1939: 356).

14. Moeran (1993).

15. Hower (1939: 346).

16. It is in order to avoid costly lay-offs of agency staff in the event of the loss of a major account that agencies in the United States contract out more specialized tasks like research and production (Tellis 1998: 71), although, in typical Japanese style, Asatsu also did this.

17. Agency commission rates in Japan range from the standard 15 per cent of the gross cost of all expenditures on behalf of a client downwards to as little as 5 per cent (although senior managers in Asatsu said that it was 'impossible' to work at less than 7.5 per cent). We might note here that the overall economic situation tends to determine commission rates. When the economy is buoyant and there is a healthy demand for advertising, top commission rates are more likely

than when there is a fall-off in demand and advertisers are able to beat down agency rates.

18. For further discussion and examples of agency-media relations, see Moeran (1996a: 173–4, 249–50, 263).

19. For further activities of this nature, see Moeran (2001).

20. Kumon (1992).

21. As we saw in the account team's worrying over the tag line that was so loved by Oba, Frontier's senior manager and decision-maker, such personal relations are often carried over into the contents of advertisements themselves, where certain words and/or images may be suggested by an agency precisely because they are known to appeal to the private taste of the client's product manager, or other decision-maker (see Schudson 1984: 44; Moeran 1996a: 89).

22. Murakami and Rohlen (1992: 77).

23. In his comparison of English Electric and Hitachi, Ronald Dore (1973: 225) suggests that the Japanese system of organization is more flexible in its lower, and more rigid in its higher, levels. This is probably related to an organization's employment practices and the deployment of different types of (permanent, non-permanent, temporary and seasonal) workers.

24. Cf. Tellis (1998: 74).

25. To help readers compare this situation with an American agency, let me add here that in 1998 Asatsu-DK's capitalized billings amounted to approximately US$2.5 billion – more or less the same as those in the US of the agencies, Leo Burnett and Bozell.

26. Dore (2000).

27. See Moeran (1996a: 110–16).

28. See, for example, Sugimoto (1997: 79–87).

29. Clark (1979).

30. The terms are those first used by Pierre Bourdieu (1984) in his social critique of the judgement of taste and discussion of distinction.

31. Jones (1997: 136).

32. Here I follow Bourdieu's argument (1993: 76) that we need to look beyond the *apparent* producer or author of cultural goods to the hidden question of what authorizes the author to do as s/he does.

33. cf. Jackall and Hirota (2000: 90–103).

34. Indeed, John Philip Jones (1998: 4) has suggested that the competing account rule inhibits agency growth and points out that Japan is a country of many large agencies precisely because clients do not object to their handling competitive businesses.

Chapter 3

1. Schwartzman (1989).
2. Malefyt (2003).
3. Boden (1994: 1).
4. Turner (1981: 142).
5. Czarniawska (1997: 71).
6. Boden (1994: 8).
7. Schwartzman (1993: 44).
8. Boje (1991: 106).
9. Benjamin (1969: 86).
10. Cf. Benjamin (1969: 87); Gabriel (2000: 27–9).
11. Boje (1991: 107).
12. Watson (2001); Moeran (2005a).
13. Boden (1994).
14. The classificatory scheme proposed here is not entirely satisfactory. As we shall soon have occasion to note, 'there are perennial dangers in the application of any classification scheme' (Van Maanen 1988: 8), but I need a peg, at least provisionally, on which to hang my Kawakubo-like ethnographic material.
15. Martin et al. (1983).
16. Gabriel (2000: 191).
17. Gabriel (2000: 197).
18. Cf. Czarniawska (1997: 46).
19. This particular example would seem to be typical of the advertising industry worldwide (cf. Hower 1939: 231).
20. Ogilvy (1983: 16); Rothenberg (1994: 117).
21. This is one of many complete narratives found in *Tales of the Past*, since it contains an abstract ('There was a prestigious...'); orientation ('I was detailed...'); complicating action ('I spotted a rival agency's plan...'); evaluation ('I think I must have got most of it right...'); resolution ('The AE...used what I told him...'); and coda ('We won the account') (Labov 1977: 370).
22. Gardner (1955: 56) quoted in Barry and Elmes (1997: 433).
23. cf. Jones (1999: 138, 145).
24. At 8.30 a.m. on the first Monday of the month, Masao Inagaki would stand up in the Agency's largest meeting room and, in the presence of some 400 or more employees, proceed to give a succinct summary of trends in the world economy over the previous month, how – for example – a recent rise in the price of crude oil would impact upon international trade, what effect this would have on certain sectors of the Japanese economy, how such effects would in turn influence clients' advertising expenditures, and what Asatsu might expect to gain or lose as a result. Here the aim once again was to help employees think strategically about how to

position the Agency in a competitive niche that would ensure future growth and prosperity for all concerned.

25. Kaitaki (1987); McCracken (1989); Miciak and Shanklin (1994); O'Mahoney and Meenaghan (1997–98).

26. Agrawal and Kamakura (1995); Mathur et al. (1997).

27. Barry and Elmes (1997: 444).

28. Ibid., p. 432.

29. See, for example, Brinton (1993); Roberts (1994).

30. E.g. Boje (1995).

31. Czarniawska (1997: 18).

32. Boden (1994).

33. Anderson (1983).

34. Bourdieu (1993).

35. Gabriel (2000: 240).

36. Boje (1991); (cf. Gabriel 2000: 20).

37. Gabriel (2000: 239).

38. E.g. Fjellman (1992: 299–318); Negus (1992); Boje (1995).

39. Schwartzman (1993: 44).

40. Ogilvy (1983: 44).

41. Ibid., 22–3.

42. Boje (1995: 1027) notes that the process of storyboarding was pioneered in animation by the artist Webb Smith, working for Disney, in about 1931.

43. Schwartzman (1993: 36).

44. Boje (1991: 106).

45. Boden (1994: 8).

46. Boje (1995).

47. Ibid., p. 1030.

48. Czarniawska (1997: 41); cf. Herrnstein Smith (1981).

49. Boje (1995: 1002).

50. Boje (1991: 124).

51. Hymes (1962).

52. Martin et al. (1983).

Chapter 4

1. Goffman (1969).

2. Turner (1988: 81).

3. Ibid., p. 23.

4. Ibid., p. 24.

5. Ibid., p. 25.

6. Goffman (1969: 28).

7. Ibid., pp. 232–3.

8. Ibid., p. 36.

9. Ibid., p. 109; see also Moeran (2005a: Chapter 2).

10. Turner (1988: 26).

11. Malinowski (1922: 85); Baudrillard (1981: 116); Smith (1989: 108–9).

12. Goffman (1969: 126).

13. Smith (1989: 112).

14. Goffman (1969: 40).

15. Smith (1989: 116–25).

16. Malefyt (2003: 149–51).

17. Goffman (1969: 52).

18. McCreery (2001: 162).

19. Goffman (1969: 52).

20. Appadurai (1986: 21).

21. Baudrillard (1981: 117).

22. Malinowski (1922: 98–9).

23. Lane (1984: 86).

24. Baudrillard (1981: 116–17); Smith (1989: 32).

25. Malinowski (1922: 89); Smith (1989: 79).

26. Smith (1989: 157).

27. Turner (1988: 33).

28. Ibid., p. 105.

29. Ibid., p. 34.

30. Ibid., p. 75.

31. cf. McCreery (2001: 156).

32. Turner (1988: 76).

33. Ibid., pp. 34–5.

34. Ibid., p. 42.

35. Ibid., p. 147.

36. Ibid., p. 92.

37. Ibid., p. 74.

38. Ibid., p. 98.

39. Ibid., p. 46.

40. As Peter Mayle (1990: 7) observes, 'in advertising, the client can mean one individual, or it can be used in the collective sense to embrace the small herd which will from time to time visit the agency for important meetings.'

41. Goffman (1969: 108).

42. Ibid.

43. Ibid., p. 97.

44. Bourdieu (1993: 79).

45. Goffman (1969: 145).

46. Ibid., p. 146.

47. Ibid., p. 32.

48. Ibid., pp. 20–1. Here Goffman basically says word for word what is going on in Japanese social interaction, even though he is talking about American society. By so doing, he unwittingly shatters the numerous 'cultural' explanations of the workings of Japanese social organization (e.g. Nakane 1970).

49. Ibid., p. 37.

50. Ibid., pp. 32–5.

51. Ibid., p. 84.

52. Jackall and Hirota (2000: 96).

53. Goffman (1969: 55).

54. Ibid., p. 85.

55. Ibid., p. 88.

56. Ibid.

57. Ibid.

58. Ibid., p. 14.

59. Ibid., pp. 168–9.

60. Ibid., p. 129.

61. Ibid., p. 187.

62. Ibid., pp. 130–1.

63. For instance, Barthes (1977); Clark (1988); Williamson (1978).

64. See Moeran (1996a).

65. cf. Jackall and Hirota (2000: 111).

66. Goffman (1969: 141).

67. Ibid., pp. 141–3.

68. Ibid., p. 141.

69. cf. Jackall and Hirota (2000: 95).

70. Goffman (1969: 29).

Chapter 5

1. Frank (1997).

2. Tahiro (1992).

3. Paul Hirsch (1972: 642–4) also discusses the unpredictable nature of cultural industries (cf. also Becker 1982: 122–4).

4. Caves (2000).

5. Hirsch (1972: 641).

6. Burnett (1971: 14).

7. Exceptions may be found in Moeran (1996a), Mazzarella (2001) and McCreery (2001) .

8. Bullmore (1999: 52).

9. Cf. Mayer (1991: 75–6).

10. E.g. Mayer (1958: 29); Young (1990: 19).

11. Young (1990: 19).

12. Palmer is generally recognized as the first advertising agent in the United States. N.W. Ayer & Son eventually took over what was left of his business (Hower 1939: 13).

13. Hower (1939: 92–7); Moeran (1996a: 64–5).

14. Hower (1939: 222).

15. The nearest I have come so far to this recognition is Claude Hopkins's (1998a: 41) comment regarding his own shift from bookkeeping to sales:

> A bookkeeper is an expense. In every business expenses are kept down. I could never be worth more than any other man who could do the work I did. The big salaries were paid to salesmen, to the men who brought in orders, or to the men in the factory who reduced the costs. They showed profits, and they could command a reasonable share of those profits. I saw the difference between the profit-earning and the expense side of the business, and I resolved to graduate from the debit class.

16. Jackall and Hirota (2000: 93).

17. Burnett (1971: 57).

18. Frank (1997: Chapter 3); Jackall and Hirota (2000: Chapter 3).

19. Hopkins (1998b).

20. Jackall and Hirota (2000: 73).

21. Frank (1997: 35–6, 95–6).

22. Clark (1988: 52).

23. Mayer (1958).

24. Frank (1997: 125).

25. Campaigns for Volkswagen, Avis, El Al, and other at the time less well-known clients are now part of the American Creative Revolution folklore (cf. Frank 1998: 60–73; Jackall and Hirota 2000: 76–8).

26. Frank (1997: 56).

27. Cf. Marchand (1985: 48). For the most part, this property of creative industries is limited to two audiences: client or sponsor and consumers. However, many cultural productions (including advertising, publishing, fashion shows and films) also address as a third audience those working in the industry in question. Some advertising campaigns, too, like that discussed for contact lenses in a Japanese advertising agency (Moeran 1996a: Chapter 4), address more than one target audience. Hence my use of a *multiple* rather than *double audience* property.

28. Frank (1997: 113).

29. Jackall and Hirota (2000: 95).

30. Frank (1997: 96).

31. Caves (2000: 4).

32. The Creative Revolution thus effectively underlined James Webb Young's (1990: 167) observation that 'the power of persuasion is a commodity that will always be marketable.'

33. Jackall and Hirota (2000: 98).

34. Lears (1994).

35. Frank (1997: 85).

36. Ibid., p. 90.

37. Cf. Arlen (1981: 14); Mayle (1990: 45).

38. Itoi (1992: 17, 19).

39. Sekizawa (1992: 5). Leo Burnett (1971: 29) also says that copywriters should not imagine that their sole function is to sit behind a typewriter. They should be curious and prepared to do other jobs.

40. Moeran (2000).

41. Ivy (1989: 34–8).

42. Laird (1998: 314–15).

43. Cf. Hower (1939: Chapter XII).

44. Adorno and Horkheimer (1973); Hirsch (1972).

45. Wolff (1981: 24).

46. Clark (1988: 53).

47. Bullmore (1999: 56).

48. Odagiri (1992: 111).

49. 180 people in the case of an automobile advertising campaign produced by Asatsu. As McCreery (2001: 155) notes, it is thus impossible for any single person to know *all* that goes into producing a particular campaign.

50. Becker (1982: 35).

51. Ibid., p. 5.

52. Hospers (1985).

53. Hausman (1979).

54. Becker (1982: 29).

55. Sekizawa (1992: 82). Bullmore (1999) disagrees: the aim of advertising is to induce a favourable impression in the consumer's mind that will then be translated into sales.

56. Fukuda (1992: 143).

57. Ogilvy (1983: 10).

58. Burnett (1971: 72–3).

59. Odagiri (1992: 117).

60. Hopkins (1998a: 72).

61. Tahiro (1992: 83–4).

62. Umeki (1992: 267).

63. Hopkins (1998a: 83–4).

64. Burnett (1971: 82). Dentsu creative director, Osamu Sasaki (1992: 172),

also relates how, when working on a campaign for JR East Japan Railways in 1990, the client kept saying that it was introducing 'more' trains, that would run 'more' rapidly, with 'more' late departure times. This gave rise to a successful *More* (*motto* in Japanese) campaign featuring the singer Kyōko Koizumi.

65. Cf. Moeran (1996a: Chapter 4).
66. Hower (1939: 338).
67. Hauser (1982: 400).
68. Cf. Frank (1997: 101). Jim Young (1990: 73) seems to be an exception to this general rule, although he was writing about the pre-war period: 'Writers who demand the perfect surrounding are kidding themselves. I have always been glad that, in my first copywriting job, I had to work in a large open room, with all the confusion of a general office around me.'
69. Umeki (1992: 262–3, 271).
70. Fukuda (1992: 147).
71. Caves (2000: 6).
72. As Young (1990: 84) – among many others – points out, an advertising campaign is a 'group product':

> While one man conceived the basic idea, three others wrote individual pieces in the series; a research assistant dug up material for them; an art director dramatized the presentation; and a type man styled it. In this process the whole group cross-fertilized one another, and the resulting product is undoubtedly better than any one of the group alone could have produced.

73. Jackall and Hirota (2000: 94).
74. Ibid.
75. Goodale and Koss (1971: 196).
76. Hower (1939: 380).
77. Fukuda (1992: 149).
78. Sekizawa (1992: 151–2).
79. Odagiri (1992: 109–10).
80. Fukuda (1992: 151–2).
81. Odagiri (1992: 110).
82. Fukuda (1992: 150); Odagiri (1992: 109–10).
83. Burnett (1971: 43).
84. Cf. Marchand (1985: 39–40).
85. Jackall and Hirota (2000: 105).
86. Cf. Moeran (1996a: 137–8).
87. Burnett (1971: 20).
88. Ichikura (1992: 316).
89. Umeki (1992: 271).
90. Young (1990: 60).

91. Cf. Itoi (1992: 23).
92. Burnett (1971: 38, 41).
93. Bullmore (1998: 57).
94. Burnett (1971: 77).
95. Young (1990: 205–6).
96. Sekizawa (1992: 75).
97. Jackall and Hirota (2000: 94).
98. Itoi (1992: 21, 23); Umeki (1992: 265, 271).
99. McCracken (1989).
100. Odagiri (1992: 116).
101. Burnett (1971: 45).
102. Umeki (1992: 267); Majaro (1998: 18).
103. Majaro (1998: 17).

Chapter 6

1. Moeran (1996a: 116–20, 140–59).
2. Malefyt and Moeran (2003: 12–17).
3. Cf. Malefyt (2003).
4. Said (1978: 43).
5. Ibid., p. 3.
6. Ibid., pp. 1–2.
7. On Japan's counter-Orientalism, see Moeran (1996b).
8. Moeran and Skov (1997: 182). Such 'stylistic reference points' have also been discussed more generally by Marilyn Ivy (1989).
9. Wilk (1995: 118); and chapters by Steve Kemper, William Mazzarella and Daniel Miller in Malefyt and Moeran (2003).
10. O'Barr (1994: 198) also looks briefly at Japanese fantasy constructions of America and points out how Japanese dreams of the United States parallel American dreams of Japan. Lien (1997: 174) gives a nice example of how a Norwegian food manufacturer resorted to such visual clichés as the stars and stripes flag, the Statue of Liberty, a cowboy on bucking bronco, jazz musicians and so on, in order to promote its Pan Pizza as 'American'.
11. Carrier (1995).
12. Ibid., p. 8.
13. Creighton (1995).
14. They also had to cater to decision-makers' self-image of what Frontier was as a company. The Home Entertainment and Creativity Quotient series openly stressed and implied, respectively, the historical role Frontier had played in the development of new audio-visual technologies.
15. Carrier (1995: 8). These contingencies also included the Agency's own need

to adapt creative ideas to its market analysis of Frontier's situation and an Anglo-Irish anthropologist's views on what made sense to himself as a European (after living a dozen years in Japan and having to struggle with Orientalism during most of his academic life).

16. See Moeran and Skov (1997: 182–5). In fact, by openly advocating Frontier's technological superiority in the Home Entertainment series, the Agency was in danger of playing into the hands of 'techno-orientalists' who use the association between technology and Japaneseness 'to reinforce the image of a culture that is cold, impersonal and machine-like, an authoritarian culture lacking emotional connection with the rest of the world' (Morley and Robins 1995: 169).

17. Wilk (1995: 130).

18. Moeran and Skov (1997: 191–4).

19. On Occidentalism in Japanese advertising, see O'Barr (1994) and Creighton (1995).

20. See Moeran (2005a: 85–9).

21. Cf. Dore (2000).

22. Spooner (1986: 225).

23. Peterson (1997: 209).

24. Svejenova (2005).

25. Elsbach and Kramer (2003: 286, 294, 296).

26. Boorstin (1963: 231).

27. Williamson (1978: 170); Wernick (1991: 31).

28. Fowles (1996: 156–7).

29. Goldman (1992: 48).

30. Goldman and Papson (1996: 141–86).

31. Boorstin (1963: 228).

32. Williamson (1978: 64).

33. Baudrillard (1996: 177).

34. Kasof (1995: 366).

35. Peterson and Anand (2004).

Chapter 7

1. Geertz (1973: 6).

2. Before going any further, I feel obliged to offer a *caveat*. Although 'ethnography' is a word that is currently fashionable in business circles, strictly speaking it does not refer to a method of carrying out research, but to the writing up the results of that research. For example, this book is an *ethnography*. The case study that it describes in Chapter 1, together with much of the detail provided in the other chapters, is based on *fieldwork*. Given that it is unlikely that a purist is ever going to win any argument in this day and age, I will from now on occasionally shed my

principles and adopt the prevalent use of the word 'ethnography' to refer both to research method (i.e. fieldwork) and to written analysis (ethnography).

3. Clifford (1992).

4. Geertz (1988: 4–5); Hastrup and Hervik (1994: 3–4), Okely (1992). The issue of physical presence is nowadays questioned vis-à-vis cyberspace research on the Internet.

5. Okely (1992).

6. Amit (2000: 2–3).

7. See Moeran (2005a: Chapter 7).

8. For the record, I should perhaps add that it usually takes me about three months of intensive participant observation before the façade that separates front from back stage begins to crack. I have no idea if there is a norm for this movement from tolerated outsider to accepted insider or, if so, what the norm might be.

9. I have elsewhere distinguished between two types of fieldwork available to the practising anthropologist: frame- and network-based ethnography (Moeran 2005a: 198–9).

10. See Moeran (1997; 1998).

11. See, for example, Amit (2000: 5–11).

12. Amit (2000: 2–3).

13. Following the example of *The Lonely Planet Guide to Japan*, I have little hesitation here in recommending my own *A Far Valley: Four Years in a Japanese Community* (originally published in 1985 as *Okubo Diary: Portrait of a Japanese Valley*) (Moeran 1998).

14. Marcus and Fisher (1986: 22).

15. Ghauri and Grønhaug (2002: 17).

16. Ghauri and Grønhaug (2002: 172); cf. also Yin (2003: 1).

17. Yin (2003: 5–9).

18. Ibid., p. 3.

19. Ibid., p. 10.

20. Gluckman (1958: 8–9).

21. Ghauri and Grønhaug (2002: 10).

22. Amit (2000: 10).

23. Ghauri and Grønhaug (2002: 19–20).

24. Ibid., 10–11.

25. Ibid., 16.

Bibliography

Adorno, Theodor and Max Horkheimer 1973 *Dialectic of Enlightenment*. London: Allen Lane.

Agrawal, J. and W. Kamakura 1995 'The economic worth of celebrity endorsers: an event study analysis.' *Journal of Marketing* 59 (3): 56–64.

Amano, Yukichi (ed.) 1992 *Kōkoku no Dai-Nyūmon: Kōkoku Hihyō-hen* (*Great Introduction to Advertising: Advertising Appraisal edition*). Tōkyō: Madora Shuppan.

Amit, Vered 2000 'Introduction: Constructing the field'. In his edited *Constructing the Field: Ethnographic Fieldwork in the Contemporary World*, pp. 1–18. London & New York: Routledge.

Anderson, Benedict 1983 *Imagined Communities*. London: Verso.

Appadurai, Arjun (ed.) 1986 *The Social Life of Things*. Cambridge: Cambridge University Press.

—— 1990 'Disjuncture and Difference in the Global Economy', *Public Culture*, 2(2): 1–24.

Arlen, Michael 1981 *Thirty Seconds*. Harmondsworth: Penguin.

Barry, David and Michael Elmes 1997 'Strategy retold: toward a narrative view of strategic discourse'. *The Academy of Management Review* 22 (2): 429–52.

Barthel, Diane 1988 *Putting on Appearances*. Philadelphia: Temple University Press.

Barthes, Roland 1977 *Image-Music-Text*. London: Fontana.

Baudrillard, Jean 1981 *For a Critique of the Political Economy of the Sign*. St Louis: Telos Press.

—— 1996 *The System of Objects*. Translated by James Benedict. London: Verso.

Becker, Howard 1982 *Art Worlds*. Berkeley: University of California Press.

Benjamin, Walter 1969 'The storyteller'. In his *Illuminations*, edited by A. Arendt, pp. 83–110. New York: Schocken.

Boden, Deidre 1994 *The Business of Talk*. Cambridge: Polity.

Boje, David 1991 'The storytelling organization: a study of story performance in an office supply firm'. *Administrative Science Quarterly* 36 (1): 106–26.

—— 1995 'Stories of the storytelling organization: a postmodern analysis of Disney as "Tamara-Land"'. *The Academy of Management Journal* 38 (4): 997–1035.

Boorstin, Daniel 1963 *The Image*. Harmondsworth: Penguin.

Bourdieu, Pierre 1984 *Distinction: A Social Critique of the Judgement of Taste*. London: Routledge & Kegan Paul.

—— 1993 *The Field of Cultural Production*. Cambridge: Polity.

Brinton, Mary 1993 *Women and the Economic Miracle: Gender and Work in Postwar Japan*. Berkeley & Los Angeles: University of California Press.

Bullmore, Jeremy 1999 'The advertising creative process'. In J.P. Jones (ed.), *The Advertising Business*, pp. 51–60. Thousand Oaks, CA: Sage.

Burnett, Leo 1971 *Leo*. Chicago: Leo Burnett Company, Inc.

Carrier, James (ed.) 1995 *Occidentalism: Images of the West*. Oxford: Berg.

Caves, Richard 2000 *Creative Industries: Contracts Between Art and Commerce*. Cambridge, MA: Harvard University Press.

Clark, Eric 1988 *The Want Makers*. London: Hodder & Stoughton.

Clark, Rodney 1979 *The Japanese Company*. New Haven: Yale University Press.

Clifford, James 1992 'Traveling Cultures'. In L. Grossberg, C. Nelson and P. Treichler (eds), *Cultural Studies*, pp. 96–116. New York & London: Routledge.

Creighton, Millie 1995 'Imaging the other in Japanese advertising'. In J. Carrier (ed.), *Occidentalism: Images of the West*, pp. 135–60. Oxford: Berg.

Czarniawska, Barbara 1997 *Narrating the Organization*. Chicago: University of Chicago Press.

Dore, R.P. 1973 *British Factory – Japanese Factory: The Origins of National Diversity in Industrial Relations*, Berkeley and Los Angeles: University of California Press.

—— 2000 *Stock Market Capitalism: Welfare Capitalism – Japan and Germany versus the Anglo-Saxons*. Oxford: Oxford University Press.

Elsbach, Kimberly D. and Roderick M. Kramer 2003 'Assessing creativity in Hollywood pitch meetings: evidence for a dual-process model of creativity judgements'. *Academy of Management Journal* 46 (3): 283–301.

Fjellman, S.M. 1992 *Vinyl Leaves: Walt Disney World and America*. Boulder, CO: Westview.

Fowles, Jib 1996 *Advertising and Popular Culture*. Thousand Oaks, CA: Sage.

Frank, Thomas 1997 *The Conquest of Cool: Business Culture, Counterculture, and the Rise of Hip Consumerism*. Chicago: University of Chicago Press.

Fukuda Takayuki 1992 'Seiyaku wa kōkoku no haha desu' (Constraints are the mother of advertising), in Y. Amano (ed.), *Kōkoku no Dai-Nyūmon: Kōkoku Hihyō-hen* (*Great Introduction to Advertising: Advertising Appraisal edition*), pp. 143–53. Tōkyō: Madora Shuppan.

Gabriel, Yiannis 2000 *Storytelling in Organizations: Facts, Fictions, and Fantasies*. Oxford: Oxford University Press.

Geertz, Clifford 1973 'Thick Description: Towards an Interpretive Theory of

Culture'. In his *The Interpretation of Cultures*, pp. 3–30. New York: Basic Books.

—— 1988 *Words and Lives*. Stanford: Stanford University Press.

Ghauri, Pervez and Kjell Grønhaug 2002 *Research Methods in Business Studies: A Practical Guide*. Harlow: Pearson Education.

Gluckman, Max 1958 *Analysis of a Social Situation in Modern Zululand*. The Rhodes-Livingstone Papers, No. 28. Manchester: Manchester University Press.

Goffman, Erving 1969 (1959) *The Presentation of Self in Everyday Life*. New York: Anchor Books.

—— 1979 *Gender Advertisements*. London: Macmillan.

Goldman, Robert 1992 *Reading Ads Socially*. London: Routledge.

—— and Stephen Papson 1996 *Sign Wars: The Cluttered Landscape of Advertising*. London: Routledge.

Goodale, Jane and Joan Koss 1971 (1966) 'The cultural context of creativity among Tiwi'. In C. Otten (ed.), *Anthropology & Art: Readings in Cross-cultural Aesthetics*, pp. 182–200. Austin: University of Texas Press.

Hastrup, Kirsten and Peter Hervik (eds) 1994 *Social Experience and Anthropological Knowledge*. New York & London: Routledge.

Hauser, Arnold 1982 *The Sociology of Art*. London: Routledge & Kegan Paul.

Hausman, Carl 1979 'Criteria of creativity', *Philosophy and Phenomenological Research* 40 (2): 237–49.

Herrnstein Smith, Barbara 1981 'Narrative versions, narrative theories'. In W.J.T. Mitchell (ed.), *On Narrative*, pp. 209–32. Chicago: University of Chicago Press.

Hirsch, Paul 1972 'Processing fads and fashions: An organizational set analysis of cultural industry systems'. *American Journal of Sociology* 77: 639–59.

Hopkins, Claude 1998a (1927) *My Life in Advertising*. Lincolnwood, IL: NTC Business Books.

—— 1998b (1923) *Scientific Advertising*. Lincolnwood, IL: NTC Business Books.

Hospers, John 1985 'Artistic creativity'. *The Journal of Aesthetics and Art Criticism* 43 (3): 243–55.

Hower, Ralph 1939 *The History of an Advertising Agency: N.W. Ayer & Son at Work 1869–1939*. Cambridge, MA: Harvard University Press.

Hymes, Dell 1962 'The ethnography of speaking'. In T. Gladwin and W.C. Sturtevant (eds), *Anthropology and Human Behavior*. Washington, DC: Anthropology Society of Washington.

Ichikura Sadamu 1992 *'Copy wa doko kara umareru ka'* (How does copy get born?). In Y. Amano (ed.), *Kōkoku no Dai-Nyūmon: Kōkoku Hihyō-hen* (*Great Introduction to Advertising: Advertising Appraisal edition*), pp. 312–22. Tokyo: Madora Shuppan.

Inozemtsev, Vladislav 1999 'Work, creativity and the economy'. *Society* January/February: 45–54.

Itoi Shigesato 1992 'Akirameru nara ima no uchi: Aruiwa, idea ni tsuite' (If you're going to quit, quit now: Or, about ideas). In Y. Amano (ed.), *Kōkoku no Dai-Nyūmon: Kōkoku Hihyō-hen* (*Great Introduction to Advertising: Advertising Appraisal edition*), pp. 12–25. Tokyo: Madora Shuppan.

Ivy, Marilyn 1989 'Critical texts, mass artefacts: The consumption of knowledge in postmodern Japan'. In M. Miyoshi and H.D. Harootunian (eds), *Postmodernism and Japan*, pp. 21–46. Durham & London: Duke University Press.

Jackall, Robert and Janice Hirota 2000 *Image Makers: Advertising, Public Relations and the Ethos of Advocacy*. Chicago: University of Chicago Press.

Jones, John Philip (ed.) 1998 *How Advertising Works: The Role of Research*. London: Sage.

—— 1999 'The culture of an advertising agency'. In his edited *The Advertising Business*, pp. 133–49. London: Sage.

Kaitaki, Jack 1987 'Celebrity advertising: a review and synthesis'. *International Journal of Advertising* 6: 93–105.

Kasof, J. 1995 'Explaining creativity: the attributional perspective'. *Creativity Research Journal* 8: 311–66.

Kumon, Shunpei 1992 'Japan as a network society'. In S. Kumon and P. Rosovsky (eds), *The Political Economy of Japan. Volume 3: Cultural Dynamics*, pp. 109–41. Stanford, CA: Stanford University Press.

Kunda, Gideon 1992 *Engineering Culture: Control and Commitment in a High-Tech Corporation*. Philadelphia: Temple University Press.

Labov, William 1977 (1972) *Language in the Inner City*. Oxford: Blackwell.

Laird, Pamela Walker 1998 *Advertising Progress: American Business and the Rise of Consumer Marketing*. Baltimore: Johns Hopkins University Press.

Lane, Anthony 1984 'The last emperor'. In *The World of Fashion*, special issue of *The New Yorker*, November 7, pp. 82–8.

Lears, Jackson 1994 *Fables of Abundance: A Cultural History of Advertising in America*. New York: Basic Books.

Lien, Marianne 1997 *Marketing and Modernity*. Oxford: Berg.

Majaro, Simon 1998 *The Creative Gap: Managing Ideas for Profit*. London: Longman.

Malefyt, Timothy 2003 'Models, metaphors and client relations: The negotiated meanings of advertising'. In T. de Waal Malefyt and B. Moeran (eds), *Advertising Cultures*, pp. 139–63. Oxford: Berg.

—— and Brian Moeran (eds) 2003 *Advertising Cultures*. Oxford: Berg.

Malinowski, Bronislaw 1922 *Argonauts of the Western Pacific*. London: G. Routledge & Son.

Marchand, Roland 1985 *Advertising the American Dream*. Berkeley & Los Angeles: University of California Press.

Marcus, George and Michael Fisher 1986 *Anthropology as Cultural Critique*.

Chicago: University of Chicago Press.

Martin, Joanne, Feldman, Martha, Hatch, Mary Jo and Sim Sitkin 1983 'The uniqueness paradox in organizational stories'. *Administrative Science Quarterly* 28 (3): 438–53.

Mathur, L, I. Mathur and N. Rangan 1997 'The wealth effects associated with a celebrity endorser: the Michael Jordan phenomenon'. *Journal of Advertising Research* 37 (3): 67–73.

Mattelart, Armand 1991 *Advertising International: The Privatisation of Public Space*. London: Routledge.

Mayer, Martin 1958 *Madison Avenue, U.S.A.* Lincolnwood, IL: NTC Business Books.

—— 1991 *Whatever Happened to Madison Avenue? Advertising in the 90s.* Boston: Little, Brown.

Mayle, Peter 1990 *Up the Agency*. London: Pan.

Mazzarella, William 2001 'Citizens have sex, consumers make love: Marketing KamaSutra condoms in Bombay'. In B. Moeran (ed.), *Asian Media Productions*, pp. 168–96. London: Curzon.

McCracken, Grant 1989 'Who is the celebrity endorser? Cultural foundations of the endorsement process'. *Journal of Consumer Research* 16: 310–21.

McCreery, John 2001 'Creative advertising in Japan: A sketch in search of a principle'. In B. Moeran (ed.), *Asian Media Productions*, pp. 151–67. London: Curzon.

Michell, Paul 1988 *Advertising Agency-Client Relations: A Strategic Perspective*. London: Croom Helm.

Miciak, Alan and William Shanklin 1994 'Choosing celebrity endorsers'. *Marketing Management* 30 (3): 50–62.

Miller, Daniel 1997 *Capitalism: An Ethnographic Approach*. Oxford: Berg.

Moeran, Brian 1984 'Individual, group and *seishin*: Japan's internal cultural debate'. *Man* 19 (2): 252–66.

—— 1993 'A tournament of value: Strategies of presentation in Japanese advertising'. *Ethnos* 58 (1–2): 73–93.

—— 1996a *A Japanese Advertising Agency: An Anthropology of Media and Markets*. London: Curzon.

—— 1996b 'The Orient strikes back: Advertising and imagining Japan'. *Theory, Culture & Society* 13 (3): 77–112.

—— 1997 *Folk Art Potters of Japan: Beyond an Anthropology of Aesthetics*. London: Curzon.

—— 1998 *A Far Valley: Four Year in a Japanese Community*. Tokyo & New York: Kodansha International.

—— 2000 'The split account system and the Japanese advertising industry'. *International Journal of Advertising* 19 (2): 185–200.

—— 2001 'Promoting culture: The work of a Japanese advertising agency'. In his edited, *Asian Media Productions*, pp. 270–91. London: Curzon.

—— 2003 'Women's fashion magazines: People, things, values'. In C. Werner and D. Bell (eds), *Values and Valuables: From the sacred to the symbolic*, pp. 257–81. Walnut Creek, CA: AltaMira Press.

—— 2004 'A Japanese discourse of fashion and taste'. *Fashion Theory* 8 (1): 35–62.

—— 2005a *The Business of Ethnography: Strategic Exchanges, People and Organizations*. Oxford: Berg.

—— 2005b 'Tricks of the trade: The performance and interpretation of authenticity'. *Journal of Management Studies* 42 (5): 901–22.

—— and Lise Skov 1997 'Mount Fuji and the cherry blossoms: A view from afar'. In P. Asquith and A. Kalland (eds), *Japanese Images of Nature: Cultural Perspectives*, pp. 181–205. London: Curzon.

Mooij, Marieke de 1998 *Global Marketing and Advertising*. Thousand Oaks, CA: Sage.

Morley, David and Kevin Robins 1995 *Spaces of Identity: Global Media, Electronic Landscapes and Cultural Boundaries*. London: Routledge.

Mosdell, Chris 1986 *The Mirror Makers*. Tokyo: Macmillan Language House.

Murakami, Yasusuke and Thomas Rohlen 1992 'Social-exchange aspects of the Japanese political economy: Culture, efficiency, and change'. In S. Kumon and P. Rosovsky (eds), *The Political Economy of Japan. Volume 3: Cultural Dynamics*, pp. 63–105. Stanford, CA: Stanford University Press.

Nakane, Chie 1970 *Japanese Society*. Berkeley & Los Angeles: University of California Press.

Negus, Keith 1992 *Producing Pop*. London: Arnold.

O'Barr, William 1994 *Culture and the Ad: Exploring Otherness in the World of Advertising*. Boulder, Co: Westview.

Odagiri Akira 1992 'Business o game ni suru' (Making a game of business). In Y. Amano (ed.), *Kōkoku no Dai-Nyūmon: Kōkoku Hihyō-hen* (*Great Introduction to Advertising: Advertising Appraisal edition*), pp. 109–18. Tokyo: Madora Shuppan.

Ogilvy, David 1983 *Ogilvy on Advertising*. London: Guild Publishing.

Okely, Judith 1992 'Anthropology and autobiography: Participatory experience and embodied knowledge'. In J. Okely and H. Callaway (eds), *Anthropology and Autobiography*, pp. 1–28. London & New York: Routledge.

O'Mahoney Sheila and Tony Meenaghan 1997–98 'The impact of celebrity endorsements on consumers'. *Irish Marketing Review* 10 (2): 15–24.

Peterson, Richard 1997 *Creating Country Music: Fabricating Authenticity*. Chicago: University of Chicago Press.

—— and N. Anand 2004 'The production of culture perspective'. *Annual Review of Sociology* 30: 311–34.

Roberts, Glenda 1994 *Staying on the Line: Blue-Collar Women in Contemporary Japan*. Honolulu: University of Hawai'i Press.

Rothenberg, Randall 1994 *When the Suckers Moon: The Life and Death of an Advertising Campaign*. New York: Vintage.

Said, Edward 1978 *Orientalism*. New York: Vintage.

Salaman, Graeme 1997 'Culturing production'. In Paul du Gay (ed.) *Production of Culture / Cultures of Production*. London: Sage/Open University.

Sasaki Osamu 1992 'Ima o ugokasu' (Making the now move). In Y. Amano (ed.), *Kōkoku no Dai-Nyūmon: Kōkoku Hihyō-hen (Great Introduction to Advertising: Advertising Appraisal edition)*, pp. 166–76. Tokyo: Madora Shuppan.

Saussure, Ferdinand de 1983 *Course in General Linguistics*. Translated and annotated by Roy Harris. London: Duckworth.

Schudson, Michael 1984 *Advertising: The Uneasy Persuasion*. New York: Basic Books.

Schwartzman, Helen 1989 *The Meeting: Gatherings in Organizations and Communities*. New York: Plenum.

—— 1993 *Ethnography in Organizations*. Thousand Oaks: Sage.

Sekizawa Hidehiko 1992 'Concept work o kangaeru' (Thinking about concept work). In Y. Amano (ed.), *Kōkoku no Dai-Nyūmon: Kōkoku Hihyō-hen (Great Introduction to Advertising: Advertising Appraisal edition)*, pp. 73–82. Tokyo: Madora Shuppan.

Smith, Charles 1989 *Auctions: The Social Construction of Value*. London: Harvester Wheatsheaf.

Spooner, Brian 1986 'Weavers and dealers: the authenticity of an oriental carpet'. In A. Appadurai (ed.), *The Social Life of Things*, pp. 195–235. Cambridge: Cambridge University Press.

Sternberg, Ernest 1999 *The Economy of Icons: How Business Manufactures Meaning*. Westport, CT: Praeger.

Sugimoto, Yoshio 1997 *An Introduction to Japanese Society*. Cambridge: Cambridge University Press.

Svejenova, Silviya 2005 '"The path with the heart": Creating the authentic career'. *Journal of Management Studies* 42 (5): 947–74.

Tahiro, Satoshi 1992 'Kōkoku wa shūdan sōzo da' (Advertising is a team construction). In Y. Amano (ed.), *Kōkoku no Dai-Nyūmon: Kōkoku Hihyō-hen (Great Introduction to Advertising: Advertising Appraisal edition)*, pp. 83–8. Tokyo: Madora Shuppan.

Tellis, Gerard 1998 *Advertising and Sales Promotion Strategy*. Reading, MA: Addison-Wesley.

Tobin, Joseph 1992 'Introduction: Domesticating the West'. In J. Tobin (ed.), *Re-Made in Japan: Everyday Life and Consumer Taste in a Changing Society*, pp. 1–41. New Haven & London: Yale University Press.

Turner, Victor 1981 'Social dramas and stories about them'. In W.J.T. Mitchell (ed.), *On Narrative*, pp. 137–64. Chicago: University of Chicago Press.

—— 1988 *The Anthropology of Performance*. New York: PAJ Publications.

Umeki Susumu 1992 'Shiten o zurasu' (Shifting the viewpoint). In Y. Amano (ed.), *Kōkoku no Dai-Nyūmon: Kōkoku Hihyō-hen* (*Great Introduction to Advertising: Advertising Appraisal edition*), pp. 262–72. Tokyo: Madora Shuppan.

Van Maanen, John 1988 *Tales of the Field: On Writing Ethnography*. Chicago: University of Chicago Press.

Watson, Tony 2001 *In Search of Management*. London: Thompson.

Wells, William, Burnett, John and Sandra Moriarty 2000 *Advertising Principles & Practice* (5th Edition). Upper Saddle, NJ: Prentice Hall.

Wernick, Andrew 1991 *Promotional Culture: Advertising, Ideology, and Symbolic Expression*. London: Sage.

Wilk, Richard 1995 'Learning to be local in Belize: Global systems of common difference'. In D. Miller (ed.), *Worlds Apart: Modernity through the Prism of the Local*, pp. 110–33. London & New York: Routledge.

Williamson, Judith 1978 *Decoding Advertisements*. London: Maryon Boyars.

Wolff, Janet 1981 *The Social Production of Art*. London: Macmillan.

Yin, Robert K. 2003 *Case Study Research: Designs and Methods*. Applied Social Research Methods Series, Vol. 5. Thousand Oaks & London: Sage.

Young, James Webb 1990 *The Diary of an Ad Man*. Lincolnwood, IL: NTC Business Books.

Index